THE FLOWERING OF
Art Nouveau
Graphics

THE FLOWERING OF ART NOUVEAU GRAPHICS

JULIA KING

PEREGRINE SMITH BOOKS

SALT LAKE CITY

 This is a Peregrine Smith Book published by Gibbs Smith, Publisher, P.O. Box 667, Layton, UT 84041

Copyright © Julia King, 1990

93 92 91 90 6 5 4 3 2 1

Book & cover design by Linda Wade.
Set in 10 on 12 Goudy by Presentor Systems, Dorset.
Printed & bound in Italy by Graphicom Srl.

Library of Congress Cataloguing-in-Publication Data

King, Julia, 1943-
    The flowering of art nouveau graphics/Julia King.
        p.   cm.
    Includes bibliographical references.
    ISBN 0-87905-164-7
    1. Prints—19th century.   2. Prints—20th century.
    3. Decoration and ornament—Art nouveau.   I. Title.
    NE487.A7K5   1990
    741.6'09'034—dc20   90-7169
                                               CIP

Contents

Introduction   /   7

France   /   8

Great Britain   /   27

Italy   /   40

The Netherlands   /   47

Belgium   /   52

Germany   /   67

Austria-Hungary   /   84

Poland   /   98

Russia   /   103

Scandinavia   /   107

Spain   /   113

America   /   118

Appendices

   Selected Bibliography   /   138

   Selected Contemporary Periodicals   /   138

   Museums   /   140

Index   /   142

Acknowledgments

My thanks are due to the staffs of all the libraries I have consulted and the museums I have visited but particularly to the following: Brighton Museum and Art Gallery, Kingsport Public Library, Kingsport; Lawson-McGhee Public Library, Knoxville; National Fine Art Library, Victoria and Albert Museum, London; Metropolitan Museum of Art, New York; Museum of Modern Art, New York; Bilbliothèque Nationale, Paris; Virginia Museum of Fine Arts, Richmond; Library of Congress, Washington D.C.; National Gallery of Art, Washington D.C

I am grateful to the following people for helping in various ways: Stella Beddoe; Jacques and Caroline Charmetant; Marek and Basia Czekanskip; Mervyn Evans; Andor Gomme; Philip Granville; Mary Jacoby; Jan and Eva Kazmier; Sallie King; J. Kenneth Major; Elena Millie; Mary Pitlick; Carol Pulin; Ann Switzer; David and Averil Walker; my daughters Lucy and Caroline Wiggin and, most of all, my husband, Joseph King.

The following abbreviations have been used in the captions to illustrations:

Va: Virginia Museum of Fine Arts, Richmond, Virginia.
BN: Bibliothèque Nationale, Paris.
V & A: Victoria and Albert Museum, London.
M de la P: Musée de la Publicité, Paris.
L of C: Library of Congress, Washington, DC.

Introduction

L'Art Nouveau was first used by Siegfried Bing as the name of his shop in the Rue de Provence, Paris. This, it is generally agreed, was the origin of the term and is a useful label. The programme for L'Art Nouveau explains Bing's aims: "L'art-nouveau a pour but de grouper parmi les manifestations artisques toutes celles qui cessent d'être la réincarnation du passé, - d'offrir, sans exclusion de catégories et sans préférence d'Ecole, un lieu de concentration à toutes les oeuvres marquées d'un sentiment nettement personnel.

L'art-nouveau luttera pour éliminer le Laid et le Luxe prétencieux de toutes les choses de la vie, - pour faire pénétrer l'affinement du goût et une beauté simple jusque dans les moindres objets d'utilitee."

Bing, Julius Meier-Graefe and Henry van de Velde were three of the great men of the Art Nouveau movement; all were imaginative enthusiasts and intelligent proponents of the style, who, each original in his own way, encouraged widespread public enthusiasm. A fashionable and avant-garde style, Art Nouveau suited the *belle époque* and was fitting for the newly-rich industrialists who became munificent patrons and the bourgeoisie who bought smaller objects with enjoyment.

The Art Nouveau artists were certain it was a new art; not retrospective, not historic, not nostalgic, and therefore suited for an era of new technology, discoveries, new ideas and an expanding world. One can now trace a number of different influences. The underlying impetus was the same everywhere but it emerged differently in different places, which is why a French Art Nouveau poster looks different from a Secessionsil poster which in its turn looks different from a Stile Liberty poster, but basically they have a certain organic fullbloodedness in common and all depend on line for their impact, effect and evocation of emotion. This book is intended to be a useful introductory guide, of necessity concise, to the subject of Art Nouveau graphics, defined here as two-dimensional works of art, usually on paper, reproduced in quantity, of varying size and purpose, and sometimes including fine prints. The illustrations include a disproportionate number of posters because these are much more often displayed in museums than books, menus, calendars and other ephemera, and therefore make a useful basis of comparison; the illustrations also include some well-known images to serve as touchstones.

The Art Nouveau movement provided a springboard in all the arts for the great developments of the twentieth century.

France

During the last quarter of the nineteenth century, life in France changed very considerably for most of the population. It was an era of scientific and technical advances particularly in the fields of transport and communication. The railways more than tripled in line-distance and rail tickets halved in price; access and local roads were much improved. By 1918 more than twenty-five per cent of Frenchmen lived outside their native *département*, many of them having moved to the expanding towns and cities. The development of the telephone and telegraph systems increased international communications considerably and the growth of the popular press assisted the development of a common national culture. In France there was a general improvement in living standards, education, health and there were many social reforms.

France recovered remarkably quickly from the Franco-Prussian war, and paid Germany the indemnity by September 1873. During the 1860s industry had expanded, agriculture prospered and total shipping tonnage increased by more than one-third, resulting in a boom from 1870 to 1873. Then an economic depression began, chiefly affecting farming, France's main industry, which lasted for about two decades. Cheap grain came from America, phylloxera ruined the vines, cattle disease was rife and there were several bad harvests. Moreover, heavy industry suffered from the loss of Alsace and Lorraine. During this depression there were several brief periods of prosperity. In the last quarter of the century there was tremendous colonial

expansion overseas in Africa and the Far East. When gold from South Africa started coming into Europe, two decades of industrial expansion and steadily rising prices began. The twelve largest Parisian department stores employed 1700 people in 1881 and more than 11,000 in 1911. In 1907 (when the construction of the new store began), La Samaritaine, with a staff of 8000, symbolised the new consumerism of the rising white-collar class.

Willing to challenge many traditional values, the new middle class questioned artistic and visual assumptions, encouraged by advances in photography. As Paul Souriau, the art historian and critic, wrote in *La Beauté Rationelle*: "It seems to me that we are present, at this moment, at the reconciliation of industry and art; the two ideas of the useful and the beautiful, unnecessarily separated, are tending to draw nearer to each other again in our spirit."

New ideas appealed to the educated general public who were looking for fresh percepts and images and reacting against the historicism around them. Through reading numerous artistic and architectural periodicals, the new patrons knew of the latest techniques, and learned to care about materials, colours and excellence of workmanship. Hector Guimard's (1867-1942) motto "la logique, l'harmonie et le sentiment" is appropriate not only to his own work but also reflects the standards of many of his own contemporaries in France.

Guimard was one of the many architects who were greatly influenced by Eugène Viollet-Le-Duc.

In 1898 he wrote to the critic Boileau: "You know how far from my mind is the desire to shock; no-one was more surprised than myself to find that one can appear so innovative after starting from classical foundations. In decoration it may be that my principles are novel, but they are grafted on those already found among the Greeks, and indeed among men." He was awarded the Premier Prix au Concours des Façades at the age of thirty, on completion of Castel Béranger. All his designs are rational, logical and well thought-out, exemplifying a subtle use of colour and asymmetry ; the expressive variety and originality of the designs were not fully appreciated by many contemporaries but were of importance to other designers, both then and later.

Emile Gallé (1846-1904), Louis Majorelle (1859-1926) and Victor Prouvé (1858-1943) founded the Alliance Provinciale des Artistes (known as the Ecole de Nancy) in 1901. The applied art designs of these men and their colleagues, like the Daum

E. Grasset: *Grafton Gallery Exhibition*, 1893, V & A

brothers' glass, are more figurative and more decorative than the work of the Paris designers.

Siegfried Bing (1838-1905) commissioned much from the Nancy designers for his shop. Bing also sold the jewellery of Réne Lalique (1860-1945), the Art Nouveau jeweller par excellence. In Bing's galleries an enthusiast could buy everything for a complete interior. Many of the designs shown there demonstrated contemporary interest in Eastern art and artefacts. This interest had began some years earlier and much of it was due to Bing himself, a remarkable entrepreneur.

Bing had joined the Paris branch of his family's Hamburg-based business, Bing Gebrüder, after leaving school in Germany. The Bing family left Paris during the war of 1870. After their return, Bing re-established and expanded the business, dealing in Oriental objects.

As a result of the Dutch trade with Japan, there had been some Japanese artefacts on the market in the West for a long time but after the Japanese signed the treaty with the American Commodore Perry in 1854, there was a much greater volume greater volume of trade, particularly with France because French companies invested their capital and expertise in Japan to build foundries and shipyards and, in return, the Japanese exported to France. There were a number of establishments, like Madame de Soye's shop in the rue de Rivoli, selling Oriental goods, such as bronzes, porcelain, *ukiyo-e* prints and other *japonaiserie*.

Oriental exhibitions were organised, notably by the Union Centrale (which subsequently became the Musée des Arts Décoratifs in Paris). A very large Japanese pavilion at the Paris World's Fair of 1878 had numerous exhibits and demonstrations showing Japanese culture, art and industry. The pavilion was well-publicised and much discussed.

Bing's shop at 19 rue Chauchat opened the year of the World's Fair, selling "Curiosités Chinoises et Japonaises". The shop was a success from the start and this encouraged Bing to buy goods in Japan himself rather than selling things acquired from wholesalers; he went to the Far East for a year in 1880/1881 and bought contemporary works as well as antiquties. His brother-in-law, a German consular agent, had made many Japanese contacts while

stationed there. Later his brother Auguste took over much of the purchasing in the Orient. At the end of 1881 Bing opened new shops at 23 rue de Provence and at 13 rue Bleue. The business was very successful and Bing began selling goods abroad mainly in Holland, England and Germany.

In 1883 Louis Gonse, the art critic and collector, organised a very large, popular and successful exhibition of Japanese art in Paris to benefit the Union Centrale, writing an important book *L'Art Japonais* to accompany the exhibition. Bing wrote a highly-regarded article on Japanese ceramics for the exhibition catalogue. Later that same year Bing organised the first Salon of Japanese Painters which was sponsored by the Ryuchikai (an association for the preservation of the ancient heritage of Japan); he wrote the catalogue introductions for both the First and Second Salons (1883 and 1884). In 1884 the family (plus two managers) formed a limited company - S.Bing et Cie. - to trade in contemporary art and artefacts as well as raw materials from the Far East. The firm subsequently diversified but Bing himself continued to deal mostly in Far Eastern art.

In 1888 Bing started a journal called *Le Japon Artistique* which was intended to be a popular, commercial, visually appealing magazine which would disseminate knowledge of Japanese culture and also encourage the general public to buy Japanese art and antiques. Its fine colourplates were printed by Claude Gillot, another collector of Japanese art. In the first issue Bing prophesied that the "art nouveau" of Japan would have a permanent and far-reaching effect on Western art.

In his endeavour to encourage the cross-fertilisation between East and West, Bing exhibited Japanese art, which was displayed with work by contemporary French designers, in a number of cities elsewhere in Europe and in America. Wishing to educate young artists and the general public in France, he provided a study collection for the Conservatoire des Arts et Métiers and both sold and donated objects to the Musée des Arts Décoratifs. The exhibitions, some of them travelling, which Bing organised, followed a magnificent, very large exhibition of *ukiyo-e* prints by many artists, including Bing's favourite, Hokusai. Soon after this success, Bing was awarded the Légion d'Honneur, a signal

honour for a naturalised Frenchman. As a founder-member of the Franco-Japanese Society, he gradually became an "elder statesman" in the field of Far Eastern art, always emphasising the connections between Eastern and Western art. Bing helped with all the arrangements for the large and very elaborate Japanese pavilion, designed like a Buddhist temple, at the 1900 Exposition in Paris. The exhibition included many loans from both the Imperial collection and well-known public and private collections. As in all his endeavours Bing tried to link Eastern and Western art in the minds of the general public, particularly to encourage artists and craftsmen of the West to be influenced in the creation of a *new art* by the decorative arts of the Far East.

Siegfried Bing and Julius Meier-Graefe, the writer, met in 1895; the same year they travelled to Brussels together where they met Henri van de Velde and visited his new house, Bloemenwerf, in Uccle, a Brussels suberb. Meier-Graefe encouraged the idea of L'Art Nouveau; for instance he commissioned van de Velde to design the façade and interior of his shop La Maison Moderne which he founded in 1899 to show the best available modern design. Several well-known designers worked on the shop, including Paul Follot (1877-1941), Abel Landry and Maurice Dufrène (1876-1955). La Maison Moderne showed at the Turin Exhibition but closed down in 1903.

Henri Roujon was Directeur des Beaux-Arts, the official cultural superintendent of visual arts in France. Roujon felt, like Bing, that any distinction between fine and decorative arts should be removed. Supporters of the design reform movement had felt for some time that the traditional, historicist, official art taught in the state schools was old-fashioned and provincial in taste and style when compared with the arts of England and Belgium. The French exhibit at the World Columbian Exposition in Chicago in 1893 demonstrated very clearly that France's industrial design still needed considerable reform if it was to compete in world markets. On the other hand, French graphic designers had been producing avant-garde work for some years.

Generally considered to be the originator of the modern poster, Jules Chéret (1836-1932) was born in Paris, the son of a typographer, and trained as a

J. Chéret: *Orphée aux Enfers*, 1858 BN

They travelled together to North Africa and Italy, where, in Venice, Chéret, discovered Tiepolo, his "god" as he said.

The travellers reached Paris in 1866. Rimmel financed Chéret in setting up a lithographic studio, equipped with new English machines using large stones. Chéret produced *Le bal Valentino* and *La Biche au Bois*, which were the first of over twelve hundred posters in his oeuvre and the first French colour posters. Chéret's success was due both to his artistic acuity and commercial acumen. By their very nature posters should stand out from their surroundings, be quickly read and understood, and be memorable. Chéret understood this and was the first artist to make use of the particular qualities required for the design of a successful poster: strong colour

lithographer, while taking evening classes at the Ecole Nationale de Dessin. At this time he must have seen work by various artists like Gavarni who recorded the night-life of Paris and the *demi-monde*, in the long tradition of French graphic art. After a visit to London, he designed his first poster, for Offenbach's *Orphée aux Enfers*, in 1858. Although the black and white poster was successful, he received no further commissions and so went back to London in 1859 staying for almost seven years. During this time Chéret worked at perfecting his lithographic techniques and refining his design style. It seems likely that he saw the large, bright American circus posters in London as well as some English posters including Frederick Walker's exceptional *The Woman in White* for Wilkie Collins' book. Chéret worked for book publishers and designed theatre, circus and music hall posters in London. During his stay he met French perfume manufacturer Rimmel, who commissioned labels and packaging from Chéret and took him under his wing.

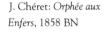

F. Walker: *The Woman in White*, 1871

contrasts and/or harmonies, dynamic lines and powerful lettering. The words imposed on designers by their patrons sometimes greatly weakened the final effect. It is interesting to observe the changes in Chéret's style from an early poster like *Princesse de Trebizonde* (1869) where there are still many details through *Yvette Guilbert au Concert Parisien* (1891) to the striking drama of *Folies-Bergère* (1893). This last poster was commissioned by the American star Loïe Fuller for her Paris début. Having started her career as an actress, Loïe Fuller went on to become an extremely successful dancer whose inventive act with veils, coloured lights and graceful movements

J. Chéret: *L'Etendard Français*, 1891, V & A

inspired a number of artists.

Chéret used subdued colours at first and then gradually employed brighter and clearer colours. Up until 1890 he used black outlines and then he changed to dark blue ink for the outlines which worked very successfully with the primary colours he preferred. From the start Chéret printed with extraordinarily few stones, very economically, which

J. Chéret: *Le Monde Artiste*, 1891 BN

accounts for the clarity of his work. He achieved his enormous output partly because he collected a good team about him at the press. In 1881 he sold the press to the Imprimerie Chaix but retained artistic control and went on to publish other artists' posters as well as his own, including the work of Berthon, Toulouse-Lautrec and Bonnard.

Chéret's formulaic designs were extremely successful and much imitated, partly because his clients found his posters commercially successful. Chéret was very astute about the commercial possibilities of his art during the "poster craze" producing special, limited-edition proofs for collectors. Chéret's colleagues at the Imprimerie Chaix were strongly influenced by his work, especially Georges Meunier (1869-1942), Henry Gray (Henri Boulanger, 1858-1924) and Réne Péan (1875-?), designer of travel posters. The critics too were enthusiastic about his designs and in 1889 his work was exhibited at the Paris Exposition

J. Chéret: *Folies Bergère*
Loïe Fuller, 1893, V & A

J. Chéret: *Benzo-Moteur*
1900, Va.

Universelle and he received the Légion d'Honneur. Manet described him as the "Watteau of the streets", according to Ambroise Vollard, an accurate description because Chéret's art was indeed, of streets, and the "chérettes", as his poster-girls were known, were theatrical, light-hearted and thoroughly appreciated by the general public.

Jules Chéret's posters are extremely important in the history of graphic art because his work succeeded both artistically and commercially, influenced many other artists and initiated important developments in lithography.

Georges de Feure (1868-1928) trained under Jules Chéret and was also influenced by the work of Grasset and Beardsley. He was born Georges Joseph van Sluijters in Paris, the son of a Dutch architect and his French wife. The family moved to the Netherlands where the artist started work at sixteen because of family financial problems. In The Hague he worked in a bookbinding company and then, moving to Amsterdam he worked in a theatre as a scene-painter. In 1891 he moved to Paris where, after changing his name twice, he settled down as Georges de Feure.

A remarkably gifted man, de Feure produced paintings, watercolours, drawings, posters and

13

illustrations, beginning his career in Paris by producing illustrations for the newspapers *Le Courrier Français* and *Le Boulevard*. He designed interiors and ceramics, glass, metalwork, tapestries, fabrics, furniture and fittings (for example the magnificent set in the Victoria and Albert Museum), and *objets d'art*.

Jules Chéret's influence can be seen in de Feure's

earlier posters. Later de Feure became interested in the work of the Symbolists and exhibited at the Salons de la Rose + Croix. The exhibition poster is by Carlos Schwabe (1866-1926) who was born born in Germany, brought up in Switzerland, and lived in Paris from 1884. Schwabe's book illustrations are extraordinary and convoluted, covering the whole page.

Much patronised by Siegfried Bing for whom he designed two rooms in the Art Nouveau pavilion at the Paris 1900 exhibition (as did Colonna and Gaillard) and much appreciated internationally, de

Feure was awarded the Légion d'Honneur in 1901. Influenced by the writings of Baudelaire and others, his work became even more delicate and elegant. It was derived from natural forms, charming and harmonious. Although he became rather difficult to work with, Bing mounted a large exhibition of his work in 1903. Later the artist founded the Atelier de Feure, designed interiors, worked in the London theatre and designed two pavilions for the Paris exhibition of 1925.

De Feure's graphic work consisted mainly of posters and book illustrations. The posters are usually flat, in subtle colours detailed, with an intentionally strange atmosphere. De Feure's most effective Art Nouveau graphic designs are the illustrations for Marcel Schwob's *La Porte des Rêves*. Much admired by Octave Uzanne, these designs are among the greatest of Art Nouveau illustrations, exemplifying the curvy line, allover design and floral motifs of the style.

Forerunner of many *livres des peintres*, André Gide's *Le Voyage d'Urien*, as illustrated by Maurice

C. Schwabe: *Salon Rose+Croix* from the series *Les Maîtres de l'Affiche*, 1892, Va.

attractive; his three earlier books are Symbolist and largely monotone, but the later books are less personal, more colourful and charming.

Brought up in Paris, Denis started as an art student at the Académie Julian in 1888 where he and his school-friends Edouard Vuillard (1868-1940) and Ker-Xavier Roussel (1867-1944) were joined by Pierre Bonnard (1867-1947); the student in charge was Paul Sérusier (1864-1927). Denis went on to the Ecole des Beaux-Arts where he studied under I Gustave Moreau (1826-1898). In 1889 the friends, including Denis, founded the Nabi group, influenced by Gauguin's paintings in the *Peintres Symbolistes et Synthétistes* exhibition. The name came from the Hebrew word for prophet. As the group's theoretician, Denis formulated the Nabis' aesthetic theory in *Notes d'Art: définition du néo-traditionnisme*, a magazine article published in 1890, in which he made the famous statement: "Remember that a picture before being a horse, a nude, or a genre piece, is essentially a flat surface covered with colours

Denis (1870-1943), is also one of the classics of the Art Nouveau style. The book embodies Denis' theories about the decoration of books in that he thought illustrations should not serve the text but accompany it, embroidering lines and arabesques on the page. Denis' illustrations are extremely

M. Dennis: *La Dépêche* from the series *Les Maîtres de l'Affiche*, 1892 (1898), Va.

M. Dennis: illustrations
to A. Gide *Le Voyage
d'Urien*, 1893, L of C

M. Dennis: illustrations
to A. Gide *Le Voyage
d'Urien*, 1893, L of C

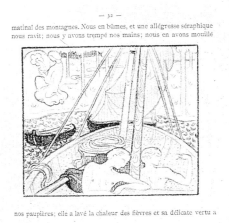

M. Dennis: illustrations
to A. Gide *Le Voyage
d'Urien*, 1893, L of C

assembled in a certain order."

Denis is extremely important in the history of art for his writings, his paintings, his illustrations and because, as a deeply religious man, he effected a renewal in religious art.

The Nabis and those around them were all intent upon integrating the arts and making them part of the total environment. One of the Nabi group, Henri Gabriel Ibels (1867-1936) was a prolific artist, a painter and graphic designer who also worked in the theatre, designed stained-glass windows, illustrated a number of books and a dozen periodicals, and drew many caricatures. In 1893 he collaborated with his friend Toulouse-Lautrec, whom he had persuaded to essay lithography, on a collection of lithographic prints *Le Café-Concert*. In 1894 he had a one-man show at the gallery La Bodinière.

Félix Vallotton (1865-1925) was associated with the Nabis. Born in Switzerland, he arrived in Paris in 1882 to attend the Académie Julian and remained in the city, taking French nationality in 1900. Vallotton was one of the first artists to revive the art of the woodcut. Unlike the gentle designs of Henri Rivière (1864-1951), Vallotton's woodcuts are powerful, with immediate impact; their influence was widespread, especially on the work of the German Expressionists. Vallotton exhibited at the Salon des Artistes Français from 1885, at the Indépendants from 1891, at the Nabis' in 1893 and at the Salon de la Rose+Croix and the Libre Esthétique in Brussels. Also he was one of the founder-members of the Salon d'Automne. Vallotton contributed to *L'Estampe Originale* which was the first collection of prints mostly in Art Nouveau style of Symbolist or Symbolist-related subjects. *La Revue Blanche*, published by the

H. G. Ibels:
*Exposition,H. G.
Ibels à la Bodinière*
from the series *Les
Maîtres de l'Affiche*,1894
(1898), Va.

F. Vallotton :*Le Plan
Commode de Paris*, 1894,
L of C

H. de Toulouse-Lautrec
La Revue Blanche,1894,
Va.

Natanson brothers, publicised the ideas, theories, and art of the Symbolists and the Nabis. Paul Ranson (1862-1909) was one of artists who worked on the magazine. He was a founder member of the Nabis and in 1908 started an art school in Paris at which many of his friends taught. After his early death his wife continued with the Academy.

Pierre Bonnard was gifted in several different media. It is said that in 1889 because he sold a poster, *France-Champagne*, for 100 francs he decided to become an artist. Bonnard's poster is clearly influenced by Hokusai, one of the artists he most admired, and by Chéret. Gauguin's exhibition at the Café Volpini was important to Belgian Art Nouveau artists but gererally speaking Gauguin's work was more important to the Belgian Art Nouveau artists than to the French. Called *le Nabi très japonard*, Bonnard designed several screens of Oriental inspiration during the 1890s including his famous

P. Bonnard: *La Revue Blanche*, 1894, Va.

lithographic version. Bonnard produced a number of enchanting and very original lithographs which influenced his use of colour later.

Bonnard designed for the stage, at both the Théâtre des Pantins and the Théâtre de l'Oeuvre, and included programme covers in his work. He designed a poster for *La Revue Blanche* and did illustrations for the magazine. For Ambroise Vollard, Bonnard illustrated Verlaine's *Parallèlement* in 1900. One of the finest *livres des peintres* its illustrations are gently enchanting, intimations of his future paintings.

Bonnard's friend Edouard Vuillard took his own work for the theatre very seriously and designed a number of programmes and sets mostly for his friend Lugné-Poë's Théâtre de l'Oeuvre. Vuillard's lithographs are like his paintings, showing one the quite, intimate side of life; he admired the work of Puvis de Chavannes and the simplicity he found in Japanese art.

One of the most influential graphic artists of the time was Eugène Grasset (1841-1917). Born in Lausanne, Switzerland, Grasset trained as an

architect. During his early life the artist he most admired was apparently Gustave Doré. During 1869, Grasset travelled to Egypt with a friend. Then for about two years Grasset was occupied in working on the decoration of the theatre of Lausanne, under the direction of the architect Jules Verrey who was a student and colleague of Eugène Viollet-le-Duc. In 1871, after the fall of the Commune, Grasset reached Paris, with a passport for one year (having visited the city earlier when it seemed impolitic to settle there), and lived in Paris for the rest of his life.

Soon after his arrival, Grasset found work as a designer of furnishing fabrics and wallpapers. In the evenings he attended drawing classes and studied archaeology, Japanese art and Medieval art and architecture. Grasset's knowledge of the Middle Ages was considered "encyclopaedic" by his contemporaries. Grasset knew Eugène Viollet-le-Duc, having presumably met him with Jules Verrey, and admired his work. Of all Viollet-le-Duc's writings, probably the most important for Grasset were the *Dictionnaire du mobilier Français*, (the most useful guide to French Gothic decorative arts), *Entretiens sur l'Architecture* and the *Histoire d'un*

E. Grasset: illustrations from *Histoire des quatre fils Aymon*, 1883, L of C

18

E. Grasset: illustrations from *Histoire des quatre fils Aymon*, 1883, L of C

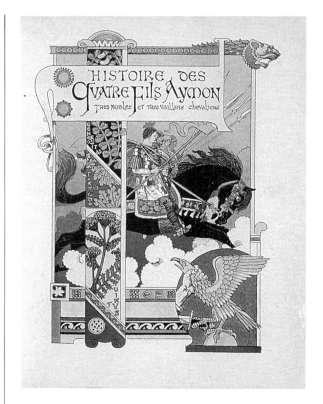

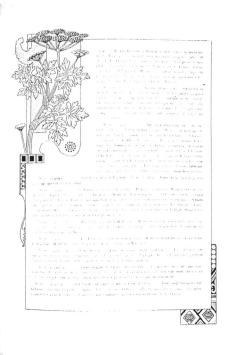

E. Grasset: illustrations from *Histoire des quatre fils Aymon*, 1883, L of C

E. Grasset: illustrations from *Histoire des quatre fils Aymon*, 1883, L of C

dessinateur, in which the author strongly emphasised the importance of drawing practice in the self-education of an artist.

Grasset's first major commission was the decoration of *Les Fêtes Chrétiennes* by the Abbé Drioux, in 1880. The ornaments for this book were reprinted later by Edouard Sagot. Charles Gillot, the printer, became a friend and asked him to design a studio for him. These designs include some remarkable furniture in which one can see the influence of Viollet-le-Duc. Grasset also designed a lantern and a chimney-piece for the Chat Noir, a café founded by his fellow-Swiss, Rodolphe Salis.

In 1881 Gillot commissioned illustrations from Grasset for a new edition of the *Historie des quatre fils Aymon, très nobles et très vaillans chevaliers*, a popular version of the *chansons de geste* of Charlemagne and his barons, with introduction and notes by Charles Marcilly. This was published in 1883 by Launette, after two and a half years' work. Gillot was an extremely able printer and one of the main reasons for the book's importance is that it was printed by a relatively new process - *chromotypogravure*

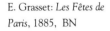

E. Grasset: *Les Fêtes de Paris*, 1885, BN

(chromolithography). During the 1840s and 1850s a number of books were printed by this method in France; most of them facsimile reproductions of manuscript which were intended to be of remarkable verisimilitude. In this aim the printers succeeded magnificently and these imposing tomes display printing of a remarkable quality and precision with fresh clear colours.

The *Histoire des quatre fils Aymon* was a turning-point in the history of book of illustration, for its imaginative and technical qualities. It was much appreciated in America. Grasset viewed each opening as a unit and the type and illustrations as essential parts of the whole. His original compositions became an endless source of inspiration for other artists. Using his extensive knowledge of medieval books and manuscripts, particularly Celtic, Grasset made the border the starting point of the design for many of the pages. Some of the pages shows clearly the influence of Japanese art in the viewpoints, clarity and use of space. The

medievalism of Viollet-le-Duc is evident and so is the influence of William Morris and of John Ruskin. Although Grasset did not enjoy book illustration (he found the work too small in scale) he did illustrate a number of books including *Le procurateur de Judée* (reissued by Edouard Pelletan) and *Balthasar* by Anatole France, the latter volume in a remarkable "Arabian Nights" style which is, nevertheless, on some pages reminiscent of the work of Walter Crane, an early influence. The *Almanach du bibliophile pour l'année 1901* was published by Pelletan and the designs by Grasset are outstanding in the series.

A man of many talents, Grasset designed wallpapers, tapestries, furniture, bookbindings, stamps, Limoges ceramics and jewellery (for the Vever brothers) which is like highly-coloured, miniature, symbolist sculpture influenced by Gauguin's *cloisonnisme*, and superb stained-glass windows. An extraordinary variety of graphic work survives. The publicity calendar commissioned by the Bon Marché in 1885 for the following year was very successful and Grasset designed a great many catalogue covers, calendars and magazine covers. In 1887 Grasset produced a book of allegorical drawings called *Iconographie Décorative*. The difference between these drawings and the twelve-page calendar he designed for the the *Belle Jardinière* in 1896 is interesting. The calendar is clearly influenced by Kate Greenaway but line is all-important. The colours are subtle and unusual, and while the girls are close to the picture plane, there is a feeling of the space beyond them, albeit stylised.

The publishers of the *Revue Illustrée*, the first French magazine to be printed in colour, commissioned Grasset, whose work they had often used, to design a new title for the magazine. The colophon Grasset did for Larousse is probably his best-known design. In 1897 Grasset was asked to design a new typeface by Georges Peignot et fils, a well-known Parisian type-foundry, and casting began the next year. 'Grasset' was an interesting, innovative design which influenced the typographical work of George Auriol (1863-1938), among others. Auriol (Jean-Georges Huyot) was a gifted and versatile designer; his 'Auriol' alphabet was the most successful Art Nouveau type design. Auriol worked on several periodicals as well as being

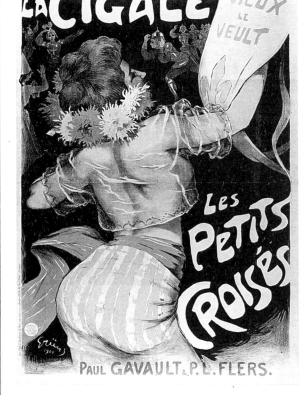

J. A. Grün: *La Cigale Les Petits Croisés*, 1900, Va.

A. L. Willette: *Caçao Van Houten* from the series *Les Maîtres de l'Affiche*, 1893 (1896), Va.

editor of *Le Chat Noir*, and illustrated several books himself and in collaboration with others.

In 1899 Grasset, Mucha and Chéret were described as the three leading poster artists of the time. Grasset designed a great many posters on splendidly varied subjects. The first, *Les Fêtes de Paris* of 1885 is much more crowded than later designs. The composition of *Librairie Romantique* was ultimately derived from Japanese art. *L'Odéon* was the first poster printed by G. de Malherbe et Cie (Nouvelles Affiches Artistiques), with whom Grasset worked for a long time. Although Grasset designed two posters of Sarah Bernhardt as *Jeanne d'Arc*, the actress preferred the work of Mucha. The poster Grasset designed for Harper's Bazaar in 1889 was a turning-point in the history of poster design in the United States. One of Grasset's most renowned posters was the "woolly horse" - *Napoleon* - designed in 1893 to publicise the *Century Magazine's* serialised and illustrated life of Napoleon. The poster was so successful that the magazine launched a competition

21

for another poster of the emperor, which was won by Lucien Métivet (1863-1932), not by Henri de Toulouse-Lautrec, who was one of the many artists who competed. In June Grasset's poster for *Napoleon in Egypt* appeared. In 1894 he was given a one-man show of posters at the Salon des Cent, the poster for the exhibition is one of his most attractive, and *La Plume* devoted an entire issue to his work.

Grasset was professor of decorative arts at the Ecole Normale d'Enseignement du Dessin, an independent and successful art school founded by M.A. Guérin in 1881. Paul Follot was one of Grasset's best-known pupils there. In addition to writing numerous articles, in 1897 Grasset published a book which had come out of his teaching years: *La Plante et ses Applications Ornamentales*; the second volume appeared in 1900. Grasset wrote the Introduction to *L'Animal dans la Décoration* by his pupil Maurice Pillard (dit Verneuil, 1869-1942), which transferred his method to animals. *Méthode de Composition Ornamentale* came out in 1905 and *Ouvrages de Ferronerie Moderne* in 1906.

Grasset was one of the founders of the Société des Artistes-Décorateurs, one of the original honorary members of the Vienna Secession, a founder-member of the Société d'Art Décoratif Français and a member of the editorial board of *Art et Décoration*. In 1912 he was promoted to Officer of the Légion d'Honneur. Grasset was one of the most influential artists of his time by virtue of his teaching and educating as well as his designs, which were both diverse and famous.

Paul Emile Berthon (1872-1909) studied as a painter in Villefranche, where he grew up, before he came to Paris in 1893 and entered the Ecole Normale d'Enseignement de Dessin. There he studied painting under Luc-Oliver Merson as well as decorative arts under Grasset. Most of the artists of the 1890s worked in several media and Berthon was no exception; he entered furniture designs, bookbindings, a fresco (admired by Gabriel Mourey) and several colour lithographs for the Salon of the Société Nationale des Beaux Arts at the Champ de Mars in 1895. Berthon is best known for his graphic art-posters and decorative panels.

Berthon's first few posters are clearly influenced by Grasset, for example *L'Almanach's d'Alsace-*

M. Réalier Dumas: *Paris-Mode*, 1893, V & A

(1868-1934), Maurice Réalier-Dumas (1860-1928), Henri Thiriet and Adolphe Willette (1857-1926). Théophile Alexandre Steinlen (1859-1901) who was a Swiss graphic artist, designer and painter worked for most of his life in Paris. Much of his abundant graphic work is political - he was a dedicated socialist - but some of his posters and book illustrations possess the line of Art Nouveau. His most famous poster is probably *Lait pur stérilisé de la Vingeanne*.

Henri de Toulouse-Lautrec (1864-1901), one of the great artists of all time, was a superb draughtsman, an objective observer, and unequalled as a lithographer. During his relatively short life - he died aged thirty-six - he produced a remarkable body of work: over 5000 drawings, some 737 paintings, 275 watercolours, 368 prints and posters and some three-dimensional works. Clearly he was not a dilettante, and although he did not need to work for

T. A. Steinlen: *Lait pur de la Vingeanne Stérilisé,* 1894, M de la P

H. de Toulouse-Lautrec: *Moulin Rouge(La Goulue)* 1891, V & A

Lorraine and *Salon des 100, 17e exposition.* In 1897 Berthon exhibited at the last Salon de la Rose + Croix. As his style developed, he began using the autumnal pastel colour palette and allover pattern characteristic of his work. *Les Leçons de Violon* (1898) and *La Source des Roches* are typical examples, as are *Revue d'Art Dramatique* (1898) and *L'Ermitage* (1898). From 1897 to 1901 he designed a series of decorative lithograph panels of musical instruments. A fine lithographer, he achieved very subtle colour tones and contrasts. Of the various series of panels, the landscapes are some of his most attractive designs.

Berthon designed magazine covers and some postcards, as well as posters, decorative panels and ceramics. Like his master, Grasset, he wished to create an original art without any model but nature, especially French flora and fauna, using the arts of medieval France as exemplars.

A number of artists sometimes worked in the Art Nouveau style including Jules Alexandre Grün

23

H. de Toulouse-Lautrec: *Ambassadeurs: Aristide Bruant*, 1892, V & A

base for his brilliant draftsmanship and skilful use of colour.

In 1884 Lautrec moved to Montmartre from his father's house near the Faubourg Saint Honoré and, some eighteen months later, he began selling illustrations to journals and newspapers. His paintings were first seen in public at Le Mirliton, run by Aristide Bruant. Although he showed works in several small exhibitions the critics first noticed his work at the Exposition des XX in Brussels in 1888 and his pictures were much appreciated. From 1889 to 1894 he exhibited at the Salon des Indépendants as well as the Cercle Volney and the Arts Libéraux.

In 1891 he designed his first true poster for the Moulin Rouge (with La Goulue and her partner Valentin le Désossé) for which he used four stones. This design is remarkable because of Lautrec's use of the white paper as a compositional element, the unusual viewpoint and organisation of space, and his use of line. This is the largest of his posters and is an extraordinary achievement, even more remarkable because it is his first. The poster was immediately successful and won him instant recognition.

financial reasons, he felt an inner drive to paint. For many people Lautrec's work symbolises the *belle époque* because he portrayed his own world; the *demi-monde* of Paris, the circus, the cafés-concerts and cabarets of Montmartre, his friends and family.

By the time he was ten years old, it was clear that he had growth problems and these exacerbated by two accidents. During his convalescence he spent much time drawing and the animal painter Réne Princeteau, who was a friend of his father's, gave him lessons and introduced him to other artists including Jean-Louis Forain (1852-1931). The family eventually agreed to send him to art school, and so in 1882 Lautrec joined the atelier of Léon Bonnat , a conservatively academic painter, moving to the studio of Fernand Cormon the next year. During his student years Lautrec acquired a sound, conventional, academic training which formed the

H. de Toulouse-Lautrec: *Divan Japonaise*, 1893, V & A

H. de Toulouse-Lautrec:
Mademoiselle Eglantine's
Company, 1896, V & A

Lautrec collected Japanese prints and one can trace the influence of Japanese art in the poses, composition, technique, and areas of flat colour in many of his prints. He would have known the work of Gavarni, Doré, and Honoré Daumier, the other great French lithographer of the nineteenth century. Only Daumier and Lautrec possessed such mastery of line, economy of means and subtle grey tones. Many of the themes of Lautrec's work echo those of Daumier's lithographs.

Lautrec was interested in the great masters of the past, particularly Goya, and his interest in *cloisonnisme* is manifested in the decorative backgrounds of some of his designs but the artist he most admired was Edgar Degas (1834-1917). The relationship between the two men was not entirely comfortable but Lautrec greatly esteemed Degas' work and opinions and was influenced by him iconographically; they painted many of the same themes.

Jane Avril: Jardin de Paris (1893) is one of Lautrec's finest posters. By this time his work was being lauded by the critics, especially by Marx and Geffroy. The dealer Edouard Sagot was also one of Lautrec's admirers. The artist was astute about executing prints to be published in limited editions for collectors. After the success of his one-man exhibition at the Boussod et Valadon gallery which was particularly enthusiastically reviewed in *La Revue Blanche*, Lautrec was invited to exhibit in Brussels and Antwerp. From 1894 he exhibited in London, where Whistler gave a dinner in his honour and he met Oscar Wilde. Lautrec travelled to England on several occasions and also to Belgium, Spain, Portugal and Holland. In addition to posters and special edition prints, Lautrec designed book

25

H. de Toulouse-Lautrec:
Jane Avril, 1899, V & A

In 1900 Lautrec was asked to sit on the jury of the poster section of the Paris exhibition. He did a little work but fell ill again. The next year he died at his mother's country estate. Lautrec's genius lies in his mastery of line, his use of areas of flat and striking but subtle colour and his unique instinct for the arresting quality of the design.

illustrations, sheet music covers, theatre programmes, theatre scenery, menus and other printed ephemera.

During January 1896 Lautrec exhibited at the Goupil gallery in Paris. The same year the publisher Gustave Pellet commissioned a set of lithographs (cover, frontispiece and ten plates) entitled *Elles* in an edition of 100. *Elles* demonstrates Lautrec's complete mastery of the medium and the way he extended the inherent possibilities of colour lithography further than any other artist of the time. Technically the set is a remarkable achievement; the images are bled at the edges and the toneplate is coloured. The set is the result of many weeks Lautrec spent living in various Parisian brothels. The detached objectivity exhibited in this series is one of the most remarkable aspects of his art.

The exhibition of Lautrec's works held at the Goupil gallery in London in 1898 was surprisingly unsuccessful; the only painting sold was to the Prince of Wales. His health was beginning to fail but he continued to work on his circus drawings.

Great Britain

Queen Victoria ruled from 1837 to 1901 and during her long reign there were tremendous social and economic changes; the population more than doubled in spite of the emigration of over a million people during this time (mostly to the United States), the Empire expanded enormously, new towns grew up, there were many technological advances particularly in communications and transport, political changes including the rise of radicalism and virtually universal male suffrage from 1884, considerable improvements in education, and great economic growth as a result of the Industrial Revolution.

During Lord Salisbury's ministries (1885-1892 and 1895-1902), there were many important reforms including the rationalisation of local government. Salisbury established *ententes* with Germany, Italy and Austria-Hungary and his skilful diplomacy ensured Britain a major share in the division of Africa between the great powers. The Boer war lasted from 1899 to 1902; a peace reasonably generous to the Boers effectively unified South Africa under British rule.

The Liberal majority of 1880 presaged much social and economic change. The boom of the early 1870s was replaced by a steady expansion in most industries apart from agriculture, which experienced a slump from 1879-94 as a result of a series of bad harvests and the import of cheap American corn, South American beef and Danish bacon. Until World War I Great Britain was pre-eminent in the world's textile industry, as well as in coal-mining and shipping. A

Anon: *Seltzbach mineral water*, 1899, V & A

shift in population away from the country to rapidly growing cities was aided by the expanding transport system. Greater London grew by over 100,000 a year during the last quarter of the century; the population

27

D. Hardy: A *Gaiety Girl*
1894, V & A

Inspired by John Ruskin (1819-1900), William Morris (1834-96) and his associates questioned the prevailing doctrine of "Art for Art's sake", and reacted against the nineteenth-century machine age. Morris said: "Have nothing in your houses that you do not know to be useful, or believe to be beautiful." The folio edition of *The Works of Geoffrey Chaucer*, a joint venture of William Morris and Edward Burne-Jones (1833-98), is of great importance. Begun in 1892, it was published in June 1896 by the Kelmscott Press. Burne-Jones designed the illustrations and Morris the initials, borders, and Troy typeface. Each opening is treated as a single unit and the book is a magnificent work of art. It was oversubscribed before printing and has had incalculable influence on Western book design ever since.

Morris and other leaders of the Arts and Crafts movement always maintained that designers should themselves be able to make the functional objects

was over 5 million by the Jubilee of 1887 and nearly 7 million by 1910.

Both in London and the provinces, department stores (including Whiteley's, the "Universal Provider") expanded as did chains of stores like Sainsbury's and Lipton's. Public transport improved in London and sport and entertainment flourished, especially the music halls and theatres. The theatre posters of Dudley Hardy (1867-1922) were very successful, especially *A Gaiety Girl* (1894), influenced by Chérct, and *The Geish*, reminiscent of Monet's *La Japonaise*. Many new magazines and newspapers appeared (including in 1911 the first Labour daily paper), some of which still survive. Numerous books on the arts were published, reflecting contemporary interests. This lively atmosphere in which old ideas were questioned and new concepts explored derived from fundamental social, economic and political changes of the time.

D. Hardy:*The Geisha c.*
1892, L of C

28

D. Hardy: *A Gaiety Girl c.* 1894, V & A

they designed and that the artefacts should be fitted to the buildings for which they were intended. This extended Ruskin's idea that art and life should be thought of as an integrated whole. Walter Crane (1845-1915) said the aim of the Arts and Crafts movement was to turn "our artists into craftsmen and our craftsmen into artists".

Crane was a prolific and successful designer and illustrator. The son of a Liverpool artist, he trained as a wood engraver in London after the family moved there. His early works were influenced by the Pre-Raphaelites and then, like so many others, he became interested in the art of Japan, after receiving

N. Keene:
Monmouthshire
Evening Post c., 1909,
V & A

a gift of some Japanese prints, and perhaps seeing the numerous Japanese objects in the International Exhibition of 1862. Crane was also influenced by Edward William Godwin (1833-86), a close friend of Whistler (1834-1903) and a pioneer of Anglo-Japanese design. An architect, Godwin also designed

29

later there developed from a reading-class held by Charles Robert Ashbee in the East End the co-operative Guild of Handicraft. In time the Guild moved to Chipping Campden in Gloucestershire.

A characteristic positive line can be seen in many of Crane's early works. During the 1880s his drawing line became more Art Nouveau in style, as shown in the flowing rhythms of the *Household Stories of the Brothers Grimm*. Crane was always interested in early manuscripts and printed books, especially herbals, and on *The Sirens Three* the influence of William Blake is added. During 1885 the story was serialised in *The English Illustrated Magazine* (a magazine started by Macmillan's to rival contemporary American magazines). William Blake was an important influence on the art of Burne Jones, Selwyn Image, Rossetti and Mackmurdo as well as on Crane's.

In the forty colour-lithographed pages of *Flora's Feast, A Masque of Flowers* (1889), the first of Crane's numerous flower books, the "curve, a swirl and a blob" of Art Nouveau are clearly visible. There

furniture, interiors and for the theatre, being a prolific writer and a design reformer. Another strong influence on Crane was the printer Edmund Evans (1826-1906), who both taught and encouraged him, acting as his artistic agent on occasion.

There were a number of handicrafts societies appearing at the time. In March 1884 Crane and Lewis Day founded the Art-Workers' Guild. This was two years after Arthur Mackmurdo had established the Century Guild, and the same year the Home Arts and Industries Association was founded to encourage rural handicraft workers. Crane was later the first president of the Arts and Crafts Exhibition Society, an outgrowth of the XV Group which held its final exhibition in 1888. Sometime

F. Brangwyn: *The Studio*,
V & A

from October 1891 after his retrospective exhibition
(at the Fine Art Society in London, which later
toured Europe and America). At this time he
became well-known on the Continent, partly
because he was much featured in *The Studio*. In 1895
Bing showed Crane's work in the first Salon de l'Art
Nouveau although his designs were not included in
the exhibition of *L'Art Nouveau* at the Grafton
Galleries. In 1899 the works displayed included a set
of stained-glass windows designed by Frank
Brangwyn (1867-1943), a successful mural-painter
and etcher, who was born and trained in Belgium.
Henry van de Velde, Georges Lemmen, Jan Toorop
and G. W. Dijsselhof were among Crane's admirers.
In 1897 Crane was made an honorary member of the
Vienna Secession. In 1900 he went to Hungary for a
large exhibition of his work which subsequently
moved to Vienna and then to Turin for the 1902
exhibition. Crane planned the decorations for the
Paris exhibition of 1914 (which succeeded the

are more swirling designs in the illustrations for
Spenser's *Faerie Queene* (1894-7), which were
admired by other designers, including Percy
Macquoid (1852-1925).

Crane's influence was probably wider than that of
William Morris because of the great variety, sheer
quantity and ready availability (because printed in
large runs) of his work. An example of this may be
seen in the influence of the "toy-books" which
introduced the Aesthetic Movement to a wide
readership on both sides of the Atlantic. His few
posters are interesting and detailed. Crane praised
the pictorial poster as "the most original, flourishing
and vigorous type of popular art existing", albeit
ephemeral. He was appointed Director of Design at
the Manchester School of Art in 1893 and his
lectures there were printed in book form as *The Bases
of Design* (1898) and *Line and Form* (1900). Both
volumes were standard textbooks for many years.

Crane visited the United States for some months

F. Brangwyn: *L'Art
Nouveau*, 1900, L of C

D. G. Rossetti: *A Pre-Raphaelite Collection*, 1898, L of C

Ghent exhibition of 1913). His plans were finally used in 1925, ten years after Crane's death.

Robert Anning Bell (1863-1933), one of Crane's pupils, whose graphic work was influenced by Crane and by the Kelmscott Press books as well, later went on to produce some very interesting designs in other media.

Aubrey Beardsley (1872-98) was one of the best-known of all the Art Nouveau graphic artists. Joseph Pennell referred to him as: "an artist whose work is quite as remarkable in its execution as in its invention; a very rare combination". He went on to say that "most interesting of all is his use of the single line, with which he weaves his drawings into an harmonious whole, joining extremes and reconciling what might be oppositions - leading, but not forcing, you properly to regard the concentration of his motive. In his blacks, too, he has obtained a singularly interesting quality, and always disposes

A. Beardsley: *Isolde*, c. 1898, V & A

32

them so as to make a very perfect arabesque."

Walter Crane, who once described Art Nouveau as a "strange, decorative disease", disliking the cult of the ugly with which he felt it was imbued, wrote objectively of Aubrey Beardsley, describing him as a "remarkable designer", but he clearly felt antipathetic towards his work.

Beardsley's artistic talent was recognised and encouraged while he was still at Brighton Grammar School. Although he went into an insurance office and had briefly worked in a surveyor's office, by August 1892, emboldened by Edward Burne-Jones's encouragement, he decided to become an artist. His only formal training was Frederick Brown's evening classes at the Westminster School of Art. Through Frederick Evans, Beardsley met John Dent, the publisher, who commissioned an illustrated edition

ISOLDE

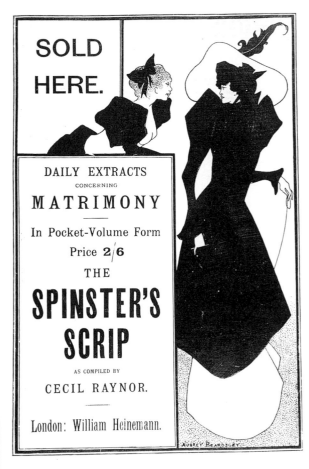

A. Beardsley: *The Spinsters Scrip*, 1894, V & A

result he received various commissions and a contract for illustrating the English version of Oscar Wilde's *Salome*. These illustrations include magnificent, sophisticated drawings like *The Peacock Skirt* which, although it shows the influence both of Whistler's Peacock Room and of Japanese prints, is a remarkable tour de force. Beardsley uses a spare, economical line which is rich because of the contrast between black and white. Eighteenth-century engravings were very popular at this time; many people collected them, they commanded high prices and the images were widely-known. A number of Beardsley's drawings, such as the various toilette scenes, echo such French engravings.

Early in 1894 Beardsley became the art editor of a new quarterly publication, The Yellow Book. The first four numbers were extremely successful and contain some of Beardsley's best work, including *Garons de Café* and *Madame Réjane*. These and the *Salome* illustrations soon became known throughout

A. Beardsley: *The Yellow Book*, 1894, V & A

of Malory's *Le Morte d'Arthur* which came out in 1893. William Morris was annoyed about the book's similarities to those of the Kelmscott Press. Dent was using the latest methods of mass-reproduction which Beardsley understood and accepted fully. Over the months it took to draw more than 350 separate illustrations and vignettes, Beardsley's style matured and simplified.

The earliest artistic influences on Beardsley were the Italian Renaissance, especially the work of Botticelli and the prints of Mantegna, the work of Burne-Jones, and Japanese prints and designs. Later he became interested in the Greek vases at the British Museum. It is possible that he knew the various books about Celtic art.

Joseph Pennell's enthusiastic article in the first volume of *The Studio* brought Beardsley acclaim as did his own illustrations and the cover design. As a

magazine only lasted for eight issues. Beardsley was illustrating various classics at this time including Ben Jonson's *Volpone* and Aristophanes' *Lysistrata*. Also he was illustrating his own work including the *Ballad of a Barber*. In 1897 *A Book of Fifty Drawings by Aubrey Beardsley* appeared. Beardsley died in March 1898 at the age of twenty-five, having converted to Roman Catholicism, and feeling that he had much left to do; as he wrote to a friend "I had devised such great plans". His was a genius whose influence is still abroad today.

Some of Beardsley's cover designs were powerful and concentrated. It seems likely that he and the Beggarstaff Brothers influenced each other. The "brothers", in fact Sir William Nicholson (1872-1949) and his brother-in-law James Pryde (1869-1941), fellow-pupils at Hubert von Herkomer's (1849-1914) art school, designed in partnership for several years. Their stark, simplified designs were brilliantly original and influenced poster artists throughout Europe although they were not very

Europe; they were published in the German art magazines almost immediately, in *Joventut* in 1898, and in *Mir Iskusstva* in 1900.

John Lane published not only *The Yellow Book* but also some of Oscar Wilde's work. When Wilde was arrested Lane was in America but, being advised that the general public held Beardsley to be "guilty by association", even though Beardsley and Wilde did not get on well, Lane telegraphed Beardsley's dismissal as art editor hoping thereby to save his investment. Without Beardsley the magazine limped on for three years.

In the illustrations for Alexander Pope's *The Rape of the Lock* (1896) Beardsley extended his range, demonstrating his complete mastery of pen-and-ink, in some of his most attractive and elegant drawings. At the same time he was working on *The Savoy*, a new art magazine backed by Leonard Smithers, the bookseller. Because of Beardsley's illness, the first issue of *The Savoy* had to be delayed and the

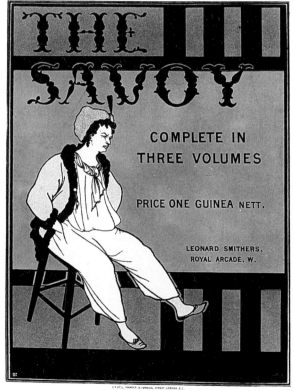

A. Beardsley: *Cover Designs*, 1895, V & A

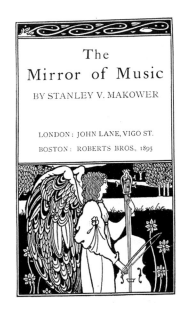

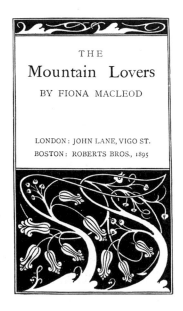

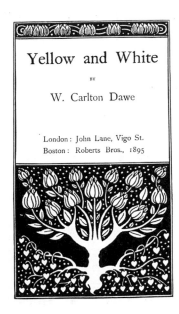

successful commercially. The first poster they produced jointly was for Edward Gordon Craig (1872-1966) as *Hamlet*. Craig went on to become a great stage designer. Nicholson taught him wood engraving and he produced a large number of woodcuts which are interesting and attractive. After the Beggarstaffs' partnership broke up, Nicholson continued to design graphics. After his famous print of *Queen Victoria*, Heinemann commissioned a series of books including *London Types*, the *Alphabet* and the *Almanack of Sports*. From about 1900 Nicholson painted landscapes, still lives and some remarkable portraits.

One of many artists influenced by the Beggarstaffs' powerful, clear-cut style was John Hassall (1868-1948), a prolific, successful artist whose work included about 600 posters, numerous postcards, book and magazine illustrations. The Brothers also influenced James Watterston Herald (1859-1914), a fellow pupil.

Charles Ricketts (1866-1931) was an important painter, illustrator and book designer who always felt, rightly, that his work had been overshadowed by Beardsley. Ricketts and his lifelong companion Charles Shannon (1863-1937) met at Lambeth School of Art. Their first major artistic endeavour was *The Dial. An Occasional Publication*, a magazine

they published from 1889 to 1897, which was strongly influenced by Mackmurdo's magazine *The Hobby Horse* (edited by Herbert P. Horne and Selwyn Image), In 1896 they founded the Vale Press which lasted for eight years. Among other works they produced the Vale Shakespeare in thirty-nine volumes, Oscar Wilde's A House of Pomegranates (1891), Longus Sophista's *Daphnis and Chloe*, Oscar Wilde's The Sphinx. Influences on the designs include Dürer woodcuts and Italian Renaissance books such as the *Hypnerotomachia Polifili*; Ricketts's style was fundamentally spare and geometrically-based like most British Art Nouveau design. An eclectic, innovative book-designer, he empathised with the text of each volume so that design and text fully complement each other. The Vale typeface was used by Lucien Pissarro (1863-1944) for various books published by his Eragny Press, which flourished from 1894 to 1914. Laurence Housman (1865-1959) was one of the artists in Ricketts's circle of friends; his book illustrations are linear and expressive but his experiments with book formats and title-page design have been influential. After the Vale Press closed, Ricketts concentrated on stage design, painting and sculpture while Shannon painted and then returned to lithography after the turn of the century. The two men formed a major

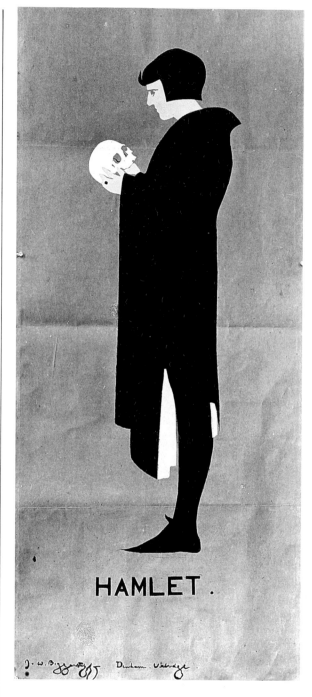

J. & W. Beggarstaff:
Hamlet, 1894, V & A

J. & W. Beggarstaff: *Don Quixote*, 1895, V & A

HAMLET.

collection which was bequeathed to the Fitzwilliam Museum.

Beardsley's sophisticated, individual style was appreciated north of the Border, particularly by "The

Four" - the Macdonald sisters Margaret (1865-1933) who married Charles Rennie Mackintosh (1868-1928) in 1900, and Frances (1874-1921) who married Herbert McNair (1870-1953) in 1899, all of whom were originally brought together by Francis H. Newbery, head of the Glasgow School of Art where they were students. MacNair seems to have been the first to experiment with The Four's Art Nouveau style although all four were clearly thinking in the same way independently; Mackintosh's *Conversazione* programme for the Glasgow Architectural Association of 1894 seems to be their first published design in the style. McNair was trained as an architect but for part of his career he designed furniture and interiors in an interesting, individual style. Later he taught for some years at the University of Liverpool. The two sisters established a studio in Glasgow in about 1894 where they practised embroidery, enamel, repoussé metalwork and various graphic arts. The Four knew of Beardsley's work from *The Studio* and were interested also by the work of the Pre-Raphaelites, Whistler, James Pryde and the Arts and Crafts Movement. Mackintosh had acquired his first Japanese prints by about 1890. According to Mrs. Newbery (writing in 1933) the Four knew of the work of Carlos Schwabe (1866-1926), probably his illustrations for Zola's *Le Rêve* (1892) for which Jessie M. King later designed a

and in 1900 the Four exhibited at the Vienna Secession to considerable acclaim. After about 1900 each of the Four pursued other interests which are beyond the scope of this book.

Talwin Morris (1865-1911) was one of the Glasgow designers discussed by Gleeson White in his articles in *The Studio*. Morris trained as an architect with his uncle in Reading and then worked on the London journal *Black and White*. In 1893 he applied successfully for the post of Art Director at the Scottish publishers Blackie's. Morris and his wife knew the Newberys and the Macdonald family (who bought their house in 1899), and he introduced Mackintosh and W.W. Blackie with the commission for Hill House as the result. Morris was primarily a book designer, prolific, able and original, his Art Nouveau book bindings foreshadow some of the most modern designs.

Another well-known Glasgow artist and book

decorative binding. Jan Toorop's painting was illustrated in *The Studio* in 1893. All these influences came together and were transmuted into the Four's highly individual style, characterised by verticality, abstraction, controlled symmetry and subtle colour.

In 1896 the Four exhibited at the Arts and Crafts Exhibition in London, showing furniture, craftwork and posters. Gleeson White, editor of *The Studio*, was one of the few people in London who appreciated their work and in 1897 he published two articles on the Four and Talwin Morris which contributed to the esteem in which their work was held on the Continent. The work they showed in London included posters for *The Glasgow Institute of the Fine Arts* by McNair and the sisters (about 1894) and The Scottish Musical Review by Mackintosh (1896).

Mackintosh continued with furniture designs and architecture, painting watercolours and designing fabrics later. His wife collaborated closely with him, painting and designing textiles and wallhangings. Frances Macdonald taught metalwork at the Glasgow School of Art from 1907. In 1898 there was a laudatory article about the Four in Dekorative Kunst,

6D THE HOUR ILLUSTRATED

THE PUBLIC SHARE IN THE PROFITS

Novel and Valuable Prizes.

MANY PAGES IN COLOURS.

BRILLIANT WRITING.

SMART FASHION PLATES IN COLOURS.

£2000 WORLD-WIDE ASSURANCE.

SPECIAL ATTRACTIONS FOR LADIES.

The Best SIXPENNY ILLUSTRATED ever produced.

J. Hassall:*The Only Way*, 1899, V & A

The work of the Scottish artists is approvingly discussed in *The Craftsman* (Volume 8). The connections between American and Scottish art and architecture at this time are interesting. John Duncan (1866-1945), taught at the Parker School in Chicago from 1902 to 1904, having directed the Edinburgh School of Art before that. Duncan was one of the contributors to *The Evergreen*, a review briefly published in Edinburgh (and London, with T. Fisher Unwin) by that remarkable polymath Patrick Geddes. Duncan was a painter and illustrator whose work demonstrates his interest in Oriental art and an unusual viewpoint. Robert Burns' (1869-1941) graphic work is powerful and positive. Burns worked in various styles and media, including pen-and-ink: *Natura Naturans* (1891) is probably his best-known illustration. George Dutch Davidson (1879-1901) was close to John Duncan, but his work was more dense and delicate.

designer was Jessie Marion King (1876-1949), who married the Glasgow designer Ernest A. Taylor in 1908. On her scholarship travels in France and Italy she admired Renaissance drawings and was also influenced by the work of Aubrey Beardsley. In 1902 *The Studio* published a long article on her work and she won a Gold Medal at Turin the same year. William Morris' *The Defence of Guinevere* (1904) and her book of flower drawings *Budding Life* (1906) are generally considered the finest of her numerous designs. King's style is dreamlike, intense and subtle, stronger than the drawings of Annie French (1873-1965), a Glasgow-born and trained designer and illustrator, which are elegant and delicate. French succeeded King at the Glasgow School of Art and then, in 1914, married George W. Rhead, brother of Louis Rhead.

C. Ricketts: *The Dynasts*,

38

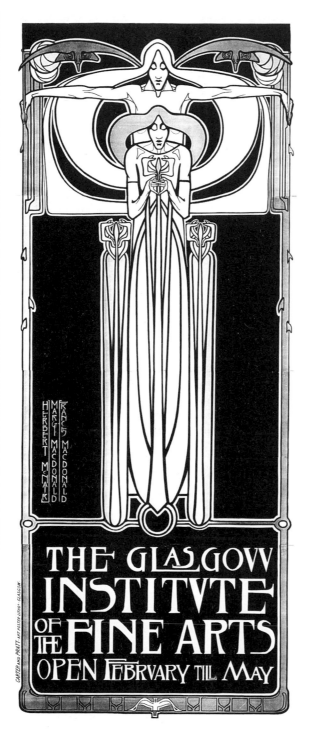

Henry Patrick Clarke (1890-1931) is often described as the Irish Symbolist. Harry Clarke was born in Dublin and studied briefly at the South Kensington Schools of Art in 1906, returning to Ireland to work in his father's stained-glass studios by day and study by night. Clarke's travels included a visit to Paris in 1914, when he met Jessie King and Ernest Taylor, and numerous visits to London, but he was largely self-taught. A remarkable individual artist, his graphic work is an extraordinary mixture of the macabre and the magical, while his stained-glass designs are rightly renowned for his use of light and colour.

The progression from proto-Art Nouveau to the full Art Nouveau style of Beardsley, Ricketts, Mackintosh and King took a surprisingly short time. It was that style which was to be the foundation of abstraction in modern art.

H. McNair, M. and F. Macdonald: *The Glasgow Institute of Fine Arts*, 1894/5, L of C

Italy

Italian Art Nouveau is known as *Stile floreale* or *Stile Liberty*; the name was derived from the London department store and was therefore considered suitably exotic for an avant-garde style. Generally speaking it was a bourgeois style and, as in other countries, not all artists and architects were interested in the movement. In Italy there were strong regional differences varying from a severely Secessionist-style to the most extreme, sinuously linear arabesques. Milan, Naples, Turin, Rome, Palermo and Emilia-Romagna (including Imola and Bologna) all became regional centres of Art Nouveau.

In 1861 Parliament had declared Victor Emmanuel II to be King of Italy. The Risorgimento cost a great deal in terms of real human suffering and in terms of money. Rome was united with the rest of Italy in 1870 and soon Parliament and the government offices were moved from Florence to Rome. The Italian kingdom established by Cavour was then well on its way to power and prosperity. In 1876 the parliamentary left came to power; but their policies were much the same as their predecessors', apart from their anti-clericalism, opposition to an unpopular grist tax and desire to extend the franchise. Umberto I succeeded his father, Victor Emmanuel II, in 1878 and in 1882 the Triple Alliance with Germany and Austria was signed, resulting in a great influx of Austrian and German money and culture.

Italian internal politics were extremely complicated but there was gradual improvement in public health, education, communication and transport - the Ferrovie dello Stato were inaugurated in 1905. Nevertheless there was an economic crisis in the late 1880s for a number of reasons including Italy's repudiation of her commercial treaty with France, her conversion to protectionism, and faltering public confidence resulting from a number of bank scandals. The expansion of railways and of steam navigation meant cheap grain from America and Russia was readily available, with disastrous results for Italian farmers. The agricultural South suffered much more than the North where industry, which had expanded particularly during the protectionist years, was mostly located. An Italian defeat in Ethiopia brought political storms and rioting.

In 1900 the King was assassinated and was succeeded by his son Victor Emmanuel III. During the next few years there were strikes, great unrest and complicated changes of government. Giolitti succeeded, however, in making a number of reforms during the first decade of the century. The general standard of life improved, wages rose, foreign trade doubled and the balance of payments improved. One reason was that emigrants, departing at a rate of about half a million people a year, were sending remittances back to Italy. The development of the hydroelectric industry of the north began at this time and, by providing cheaper fuel, boosted industry. In 1899 the Fiat company was founded. The Italo-Turkish war of 1911-2 was costly and temporarily upset the economy, but by that time Italy had

had looked at the work of both Chéret and Mucha and was influenced by Bonnard, his designs are certainly original; his posters for Puccini's *Tosca* (1899) and Mascagni's *Iris* (1898), for example, show individual richness of composition, flamboyance of colour, and originality of viewpoint. Hohenstein was born in St. Petersburg of a German family but lived and worked in Milan, where he later became artistic director of the Officine Grafiche Ricordi; he designed covers for musical scores (Ricordi published a great many opera scores), magazine covers, book illustrations, postcards, commercial posters, and illustrations for magazines including *Emporium*, the periodical which was published by the Institute of Graphic Arts in Bergamo from 1895, modelled on *The Studio*, and showed much English design, Chicago architecture and many *Jugend* illustrations.

As artistic director of Ricordi, Hohenstein encouraged other designers, among them Giovanni Mataloni (1869-1944), who was born in Rome but settled in Milan, where he worked for Ricordi as a

G. Mataloni: *Incandescenza*, 1895, L of C

advanced economically, politically and socially.

The graphic art of this time reflects the history of the country. Italy, while starting later than France or England, soon made up for lost time and some remarkable works appeared. Among the most influential books were Walter Crane's *Claims of Decorative Art* (1892), Grasset's publications and Henry van de Velde's *Le Déblaiement d'Art* (1894). The first posters were not for the circus or the theatre but for the opera; its passion and emotional fire was well suited by the drama and sophistication of the Art Nouveau style.

Rossetti drew the first lithographed poster for Gounod's *Faust* in 1863 but Adolfo Hohenstein's design for Puccini's *Edgar*, published by G. Ricordi & C. in 1889, was the first really dramatic Italian poster, and his placard for *Corriere della Serra* (1897) was one of the first Art Nouveau posters in Italy. Hohenstein (1854-?) occupies much the same position in Italy as Chéret in France. Although he

A. Hohenstein: *Birra Italia*, V & A

typographer and then as a commercial artist. At the
turn of the century there was considerable demand
for printed material of all sorts, including the posters
and programmes for the cafés-chantants which had
appeared in Italy, as elsewhere in Europe. Mataloni
worked for several printing firms designing posters,
music score covers, postcards and other ephemera
and for a publishing firm in Turin designing book
covers, as well as providing illustrations for a number
of magazines including *Emporium*, *Novissima*, *La
Tribuna*, and *Ora di Palermo*. In his posters the
lettering complements the design and the dramatic
content fits the subject; his style developed from a
very tight, detailed form of Art Nouveau, influenced
by Mucha, to a looser, more flowing manner clearly
influenced by Japanese art.

Leopoldo Metlicovitz (1868-1944) began working
for Ricordi, in Milan, as an assistant lithographer in
1892. His early poster designs, that for Puccini's
Tosca for example, are attractive but later his style
became much heavier, darker and rather solid.
Metlicovich worked as a graphic designer for
publishing firms, magazines and commercial
companies as well.

Franz Laskoff (François Laskowski 1869-1919 or
1921), who studied at the Kunstgewerbeschule in
Strasbourg and in Paris before moving to Italy in
1898, worked for the Officine Grafiche Ricordi from
1900 to 1906 and then moved to England. Clearly
influenced by the Beggarstaff Brothers and Aubrey
Beardsley, Laskoff's designs employ flat, strong
colours and his monochrome designs are very
powerful.

Among the other artists who worked for Ricordi

42

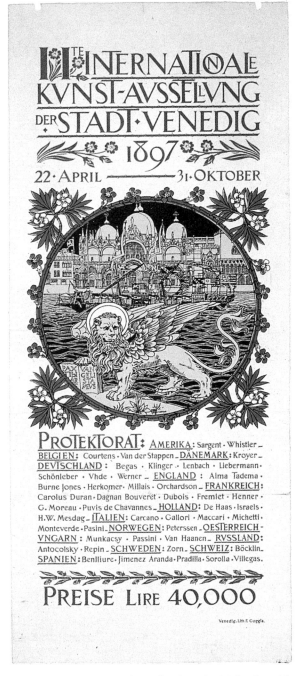

and later became one of the leaders of the Roman Secession, whose work for magazines is starkly black and white with spare, economical lines. Villa was a prolific artist and graphic designer who won first prize in the *Cigarillos Parsi* competition in Buenos Aires in 1901. Ballerio's style was prettier than that of Villa, influenced by Chéret's work. After about 1910 he worked for Chappuis in Bologna as well as Ricordi and other companies in Milan.

Many of the Ricordi artists worked on *Ars et Labor*, a musical monthly magazine. *Novissima*, directed by Edoardo de Fonseca, was published in both Milan and Rome. In Rome the group In Arte Liberas was founded by Nino Costa in 1885. Like the Pre-Raphaelites and William Morris, whom they much admired, the group wished to return to traditional values in art. The paintings of Aristide Sartorio (1860-1932), a member of the group, are reminiscent of those of William Blake. Edoardo Gioia's work, on the other hand, looks back to the Italian Renaissance. The important magazine *Arte Italiana Decorativa ed Industriale*, published in Rome and Venice from 1890 to 1914, was traditionally biased but contained some modern designs and was very well illustrated. *L'Italia che ride*, a well-illustrated, avant-garde Socialist magazine published in Bologna, was inspired by *Le Rire* and *La Revue Blanche*.

One of the artists who worked on *L'Italia che ride* was Marcello Dudovich (1878-1962). Born in Trieste, he was self-taught and had a long, successful career. After an early study trip to Munich, he worked at Ricordi in Milan under Metlicovitz's tutelage, particularly on the series of posters for Mele, the department store in Naples; later they worked in Monaco together. Also influenced by Mucha, Penfield and Hohenstein, Dudovich soon found his own richly coloured, very graphic style. In 1899 he moved to Bologna where he worked for Edmondo Chappuis. The next year he won a poster competition and the Gold Medal (poster section) at the 1900 Exposition Universelle. Dudovich continued to provide illustrations for various magazines and worked for Ricordi and for Grafiche Armanino in Genoa. In 1911 Dudovich won the Lazzaro & C *Zenit* poster competition with a superb design. For three years he was a special

in Milan were Aleardo Villa (1865-1906), Osvaldo Ballerio (1870-1942), Giovanni Beltrami (1860-1926), well known as a stained glass designer, Aldo Mazza (1880-1964), and Aleardo Terzi (1870-1943), who trained in Palermo, moved to Rome in 1892,

A. de Karolis:
illustrations for *Francesca
da Rimini* by Gabriele
d'Annunzio, 1902, photo
author , V & A

correspondent for *Simplicissimus*. In 1914 he won the
DAG poster competition but returned to Italy when
war broke out.

Two magazines published in Turin from 1902, the

year of the First International Exhibition of Modern Decorative Art, were *L'Arte decorativa moderna* and *Il Giovane Artista Moderno*. Probably the greatest Italian achievements of the time were in architecture especially the work of Raimondo d'Aronco, Pietro Fenoglio, Giuseppe Sommaruga, Gino Coppedè, G. B. Comencini and a number of others; one of the greatest being Ernesto Basile (1857-1932) whose remarkable designs range from furniture to buildings including his work at the Villa Igea, Palermo. There are some magnificent interior designs of this time including the work of G. Valentini, Alessandro Mazzucotelli, Gaetano Moretti, G. Cometti and Annibale Rigotti (1870-?), whose work was greatly influenced by Mackintosh. The Secessionist strain in Italian Art Nouveau architecture was strong and influential; the early designs of Antonio Sant'Elia, the Futurist, are reminiscent of Olbrich's plans dated at the turn of the century. Sant'Elia was killed in the Great War. Among the other architects who worked in this style were Gaetano Moretti, Giovanni Michelazzi and Guido Constante Sullam.

Like a number of his contemporaries, Giuseppe Palanti (1881-1946), a successful painter, graphic and theatre designer, who taught at the Accademia di Brera and at the Scuola superiore di arte applicata all' industria in Milan, was influenced by Mucha's work, classical art and also by the Secession. Many of the paintings of the fashionable portrait artist Giovanni Boldini (1842-1931) are Art Nouveau in style. Luigi Rossi's book illustrations are strongly influenced by Art Nouveau ideas, especially his illustrations for Loti's *Madame Chrysanthème* (1887-8). Gaetano Previati (1852-1920) and Giovanni Segantini (1858-1899), especially in his last great triptych *Life Nature and Death* (1899) intended for the Paris 1900 Exhibition, exemplify the strange and sometimes desolate Symbolist Italian painting, which is paralleled in the sculpture of Adolfo Wildt and Leonardo Bistolfi (1876-1920).

The graphic works, including illustrations for *Emporium* and other magazines, of Alberto Martini (1876-1954) are equally strange; his illustrations for books and plays, including works by Baudelaire, Rimbaud, Verlaine, Mallarmé and Dante, are sometimes macabre and bizarre; the Surrealists later were interested by his work.

A number of painters executed graphic designs including posters for exhibitions; Leonardo Bistolfi's Turin Exhibition poster is a splendid example. Felice Casorati (1886-1963), Umberto Boccioni (1882-1916), Galileo Chini (1873-1956), Vittorio Zecchin (1878-1947) and Augusto Sezanne (1856-1935) all explored the possibilities of graphic art.

Adolfo de Karolis (1874-1928) studied first in Bologna and then at the Scuola di Decorazione Pittorica in Rome. In 1897 he became a member of In Arte Liberas, exhibiting with them the same year. Having won the Gold Medal at the Scuola, and having exhibited successfully at the Venice Biennale, he moved to Florence in 1901 to teach at the Accademia di Belle Arti. At this time he started working with Gabriele d'Annunzio and illustrated several of his books as well as designing sets for two plays. One of de Karolis' great achievements was his revival of the Italian woodcut. De Karolis illustrated numerous books, in a style influenced by the pre-Raphaelites, and worked for a number of magazines, including *Novissima* and *L'Eroica*, while working on several large-scale fresco cycles. Later he taught in Bologna and then Rome. Duilio Cambellotti (1876-1960) was another distinguished illustrator and graphic designer. Like de Karolis, he studied at the Scuola attached to the Museo Artistico Industriale in Rome; in 1897 he received the licence to teach in art schools. In 1898 he showed work in the exhibition of the Società Promotrice di Belle Arti in Turin and the next year stayed with d'Aronco in Constantinople. Cambellotti worked for a number of magazines including *L'Italia Che Ride*, *Novissima*, *Avanti della Domenica* and the revolutionary socialists' *Divenire sociale*. He illustrated numerous books including Dante's *La Divina Commedia* (1902-3) and D'Annunzio's *La Nave* (1913), and also some children's books, as did Augusto Maiani (known as Nàsica, 1867-1958/9) and Antonio Rubino (1880-1964). In 1905 Cambellotti began designing for the stage, as well as painting, working with the group XXI della campagna romana. He was a professor at the Istituto d'Arte in Rome from 1908 and active with the socialist movement for *Scuole rurali*.

Achille Mauzan (1883-1952), born in France, trained at the Ecole des Beaux-Arts in Lyon and settled in Turin, then the centre of the Italian film

industry. Mauzan was extremely successful and designed large numbers of film posters as well as working for Ricordi. Later he founded the Clamor agency. During the thirties he spent some time in Buenos Aires and then returned to France, working in Paris.

One of the most successful Italian graphic artists of the time, Leonetto Cappiello (1875-1942), spent almost all his working life in France. Influenced by the work of Chéret and Bonnard, Cappiello began by working for various magazines and newspapers including *L'Assiette au Beurre* and *Le Figaro*, but his long and very successful career was established particularly by the posters *Cinzano Vermouth*, *Frou-Frou* (1899) and *Chocolat Klaus* (1903) which brought him many commissions; his designs for Italy were usually travel posters.

Manuel (Emmanuel) Orazi (1860-1934) also spent his working life in France; he contributed to various magazines, illustrated books and designed a number of posters for Sarah Bernhardt and Loïe Fuller, among other people, as well as working for Julius Meier-Graefe at La Maison Moderne.

Although Italian Art Nouveau graphic art did not reach the heights achieved in some other countries, there was much interesting, individual work, and much that foreshadows the exciting developments of later twentieth-century art.

L. Cappiello

The Netherlands

In 1890 Queen Wilhelmina succeeded to the throne but until she reached her majority in 1898 her mother acted as Regent. From 1890 to 1913, the governments changed regularly every four years with only one brief exception. The political situation was much more complicated than this would indicate, however, because the power of the long-established (but divided) Liberal party was waning as a number of new parties emerged. The Roman Catholic and Calvinist coalition government in power from 1888 to 1891 was kept together by mutual dislike for the Liberals' educational policy of opposition to private, denominational schools. Trade unionists among the Roman Catholic population had banded together nationwide by 1909, as had Calvinist trade unionists. The Antirevolutionary party headed by Kuyper, and its offshoot, the Christian Historical Union, both held different views from orthodox Calvinists. The new socialist movement was at first divided between the anarchist, strongly individualistic Social Democratic Union and the Social Democratic Labour party (which eventually absorbed the Union and established its own trade unions in 1906). Extending the franchise to almost general suffrage became the paramount issue and the Liberal party split over this three ways; the most radical section became the Liberal Democrat party in 1901. During the twenty years before the First World War, much social legislation was enacted, with a growing tendency towards democratisation. The strike movement of 1903, although broken by the government, resulted in better labour conditions. In

MAATSCHAPPELIJK KAPITAAL : EEN MILLIOEN GULDEN

1917 private schools were all placed on the same financial subsidy as the public schools. Universal male suffrage was adopted with proportional representation. Women's suffrage followed two years later.

The problems of a small country (population

J.Toorop:
Levensverzekering Maatschappij Arnhem,
1900 L of C

47

about 6 million in 1910) surrounded by major powers became more complicated as Germany's expansionist policy, particularly towards the East Indian colonies, became clear; the traditional policy of neutrality became difficult to maintain and a series of pacts were concluded, while the country's defences were strengthened and the army reorganised.

The Netherlands East Indies' export trade doubled between 1900 and 1913. This was one of the two major factors in the Dutch economic revival; the other being trade with the heavy industries of the Ruhr. Originally the canals had been used mainly for irrigation but as time went on the Dutch found that transport on the canals, including a transit trade, was profitable. The government built railways in the early 1860s. After an agricultural crisis in 1885, the industry was reorganised around farmers' cooperatives. Industrialisation came relatively late to the Netherlands but by the turn of the century the traditional textile, paper and shipbuilding industries had expanded considerably and there had been greatly increased migration to the towns. As a

commercial nation, the Netherlands had much private capital and foreign investment was encouraged from this time; modern financial, trade and industrial patterns were established, including organised labour and large multinational companies.

Economic and religious revivals were paralleled by an artistic and literary revival. In the Netherlands Art Nouveau was called Nieuwe Kunst. One event particularly important for the development of Nieuwe Kunst was the exhibition of British graphic art in The Hague in 1893. During the 1880s several magazines were founded including *Bouwen Siekunst* and *Arts and Crafts. De Nieuwe Gids* was first published in 1885. Compared to the critical magazine *De Gids* it was an aesthetic, literary review, embodying the ideas of a literary movement known as "the generation of the eighties". The leaders of this movement were Willem Kloos, Albert

Verwey, Frederik van Eeden and Louis Couperus.

The great Socialist writer Henriette Roland Holst-Van der Schalk was most concerned with social and philosophical problems; the poet was married to Richard Nicolaus Roland Holst (1868-1938). After studying under Allebé at the Rijksakademie in Amsterdam from 1885 to 1890, Roland Holst was considerably influenced for some time by the work of George H. Breitner (1857-1923) whose remarkable impressionist landscapes have a strong underlying graphic quality. Influenced by Van Gogh (he designed the catalogue for the painter's memorial exhibition in 1892), the Pre-Raphaelites and Beardsley, his graphic art became decorative and linear. While he never belonged to Les XX, he was close to Henry van de Velde and Georges Lemmen and contributed designs to *Van Nu en Straks* . During the mid-1890s he visited London and became especially interested by the work of Charles Ricketts; his book illustrations particularly reflect this. From about 1900 his work was monumental, including a number of murals; he taught at the Rijksakademie from 1918 and was later Principal there.

One of the most original geniuses of Art Nouveau, Jan (Johannes Theodorus) Toorop (1858-1928) was born at Poerworedjo in Java and was brought to the Netherlands at the age of fourteen. He studied in Delft and then at the Rijksakademie in Amsterdam for two years from 1880 and then at the Academy in Brussels with A. J. Derkinderen (1859-1925) for three years. While in Brussels he was befriended by James Ensor and they went to Paris together. According to W. Shaw Sparrow, writing in *The Studio* , Toorop was afterwards ill for some months and studied Eastern religion and literature. The influence of Indonesian art, including shadow-puppets with their elongated silhouettes, and also the complicated patterns of batik, is clear in his work. The complicated, elaborate, esoteric mysticism of his Symbolist pictures inter-weaves various different strands of influence including that of William Blake. While on a trip to England with Emile Verhaeren (1855-1916), Toorop admired the work of the Pre-Raphaelites and William Morris as well as Blake and Beardsley. It also seems possible that he had looked at Celtic art; his wife was Irish and also various books on the subject were appearing at this time. In 1884

Toorop became a member of Les XX and became a friend of Maurice Maeterlinck who encouraged him to move towards Symbolism. He exhibited with them in Brussels until the group broke up in 1893, the year that his remarkable painting *The Three Brides* appeared in *The Studio*; described by Sparrow as "this odd, fantastic, sibylline production", it was widely influential, particularly for the Glasgow artists. Toorop also used his expressive, curvilinear line in his graphic work and continued to do so later in his career when his paintings were impressionistic in style rather than Art Nouveau. Toorop, Lodewijk Schelfhout, Mondrian and the critic Conrad Kikkert founded the Amsterdamse Kunstkring in 1910, an important group for the development of modern European painting in the Netherlands.

Toorop's graphic works are Art Nouveau in style, extraordinarily imaginative and original, and include drawings, woodcuts and lithographs for books, magazines and posters. *Delftsche Slaolie* (ca. 1895) is one of the most remarkable; looking at the poster one is more conscious of the pattern made by the girls' hair and less of the pattern of their dresses than is evident in a black and white photograph. Toorop converted to Catholicism in 1905 and from then on painted mostly religious pictures, which do not have the intensity and expressive line of his Art Nouveau works.

Johan Thorn Prikker (1868-1932) studied at the Academy of Fine Arts in The Hague, where he was born, from 1883-7. For several years he painted in a Neo-Impressionist style but, in about 1892, he encountered the work of Denis, Gauguin and Toorop and became a Symbolist. Thorn Prikker exhibited *The Bride* at the tenth and last exhibition of Les XX at Toorop's suggestion. In this remarkable painting Thorn Prikker was using line to convey the emotions and feelings of the figures rather than the figures themselves. Prikker designed for Arts and Crafts, the shop in The Hague, for some years. His interest in religious art is shown by the severe, passionate poster for a magazine *Revue Bimestrielle pour L'art Appliqué* and his stained-glass designs and murals were influential for later church art. He taught in Krefeld, Essen, Munich, Düsseldorf and Cologne where he died.

Numerous artists were influenced by the work of

J. T. Prikker:
*Hollandische
Kunstausstellung Krefeld,*
1903, L of C

J. T. Prikker:
*Niederlandisch-Indische
Kunstaustellung Krefeld,*
1906, L of C

Toorop and Beardsley, including Bart van der Leck (1876-1958). During the 1890s he worked at glass studios in Utrecht and then went to Amsterdam to study at the Rijksschool voor Kunstnijverheid and at the Rijksakademie in the evenings. Later he was a founding member of De Stijl.

Theo van Hoytema (1863-1917), who studied at the Academy in The Hague, was more interested by Japanese prints than most of the Dutch artists of the time. In his book designs he developed the use of an elongated format which is very striking to handle. Many of his graphic designs are immensely detailed, with strange, faintly sinister plants and animals, which he studied in the zoos in Leiden and Amsterdam. A successful painter and graphic designer, he showed at many international exhibitions, and was a member of the Haagse Kunstkring (after 1892) and of the Arti et Amicitiae association from 1893.

Theodorus H. A. A. Molkenboer (1871-1920), an architect, designer and painter, studied with the architect H. P. J. Cuypers and also with G. W. Dijsselhof and A. J. Derkinderen (1859-1925). Later he himself became director of the Hendrick de Keyser school in Amsterdam. Molkenboer designed book illustrations and some very successful posters.

Gerrit Willem Dijsselhof (1866-1924) studied at The Hague and then Amsterdam. During 1889 and 1890 he travelled with Theodor Nieuwenhuis (1866-1951) to Berlin, Dresden, Prague, Vienna and Paris. Both men were members of the Labor et Ars association. Dijsselhof designed graphics in a striking style somewhat influenced by Javanese art. In 1895 he designed the 'Dijsselhof-kamer' for Dr. W. van Hoorn in Amsterdam, which was illustrated in various magazines and extremely influential. The stylistic dominance of the English Arts and Crafts Movement is clear and, furthermore, influenced the next generation.

Theodoor Willem Nieuwenhuis trained in Amsterdam and returned there after his travels. His work includes some very striking graphic designs, including his poster for *Delftsche Slaolie* (1893), and also some important furniture designed for Van Wisselingh the art shop Amsterdam owned by K.Grousbeck who commisioned work from, C. A. Lion Cachet and other artists.

The great architect Hendrik Petrus Berlage (1856-1934), a disciple of Semper, having studied in Zurich, and also influenced by the writings of Ernst Haeckel, aimed for a universal style, but one of truth to materials and clarification of structure rather than Art Nouveau which he felt to be eccentric and esoteric. Berlage was extremely influential for the later development of Dutch architecture, for De Stijl and for the Amsterdam school of the 1920s.

Nieuwe Kunst is distinguished for its distinctive, original style, including the remarkable art of Jan Toorop, with its extraordinary quality of abstraction. Much of the most interesting work is to be found in the field of applied arts, although there are many interesting graphic designs, including some superb posters and remarkable, avant-garde book illustrations.

Belgium

The accession of Leopold II in 1865 was greeted with loyal enthusiasm from which it was clear that the monarchy was solidly established, and the King's policies generally approved. Belgium continued her policy of armed neutrality; during the Franco-Prussian war the army was mobilised to prevent crossing of the country's frontiers, by either side, and from 1887 the fortifications of Liége and Namur were strengthened, underlining the government's intentions. The Liberal party was defeated in the 1884 elections mainly because of internal divisions and there were successive Catholic ministries for the next thirty years, despite the gradual rise of socialism. After riots in Liége in 1886, the government introduced a number of reforms, including establishment of universal male suffrage, and in 1898 the Chambers adopted an act which, in effect, made French and Flemish equal languages.

Belgium was one of the most highly industrialised nations in the world as well as one of the most densely populated countries in Europe. In the nineteenth century Belgium had excellent road, rail and water communications. After the country became independent in 1831, there had been some loss of overseas trade although the government pursued a free trade policy which to some degree compensated for the loss. A desire for more overseas trade was one reason why Leopold II, from the very beginning of his reign, was determined to establish a Belgian colony in Africa in spite of popular disapproval. He focused his interest on Central Africa, then largely unexplored, after Stanley made

his historic journey across the continent in 1874-7, appointing him his chief agent, in what became the Congo Free State, later to be annexed by Belgium. Belgian colonial policy was chiefly distinguished from that of other European countries by its paternalism and its centralisation.

At home a geographical meeting-place, rich and

C. A. L. Cachet: *Sigaren*, 1897, L of C

52

J. Zon Dobbelmann:
Frères, 1898, L of C

industrialised, Belgium was culturally lively, open-minded, and interested in new ideas and the avant-garde. In 1881 Octave Maus, a lawyer, started the influential review *L'Art Moderne* and then, in 1884, the same year as the Indépendants were founded, assisted the formation of Les XX, which, under his leadership, was a remarkably forward-looking and progressive exhibition society, later succeeded by La Libre Esthétique (1894-1914). The exhibitions, lectures and concerts of the Belgian societies were vital to the development of modern art. In 1895 a

shop, the Toison d'Or, was opened by the son of Edmond Picard, one of Maus' confrères, which may have influenced Bing in opening his own shop. There were several artistic groups with salons, including L'Art Idéaliste, Pour l'Art (1891) and Le Sillon (1893) in Brussels. Almost all the great innovators exhibited with Les XX, including Gauguin, Toulouse-Lautrec, Cézanne, van Gogh and Seurat (*Sunday Afternoon on the Island of La Grande Jatte* was shown in 1887). Not surprisingly, given the Belgian interest in new ideas, the influence of Oriental art spread rapidly. La Maison Japonaise opened in Brussels in 1866 and in 1884, after a visit to England where he discovered the work of Ruskin, Morris and the Arts and Crafts Movement, Gustave Serrurier-Bovy (1848- 1910) opened a shop in Liége selling objets d'art from the Orient and from Liberty of London. A prescient man, he was an acknowledged influence on van de Velde so that his

J. Sluyters: *Gemalde
Ausstellung*, 1913, L of C

H. van de Velde: *Tropon*,
1897, L of C

H. van de Velde: Pelleas et Mélisande, 191-, L of C

work is important in the history of Belgian art and
decoration as it formed a link between British
developments and the Belgian avant-garde.
Eventually moving on from his architectural training
to designing furniture full-time, Serrurier-Bovy
exhibited at the first Salon de la Libre Esthétique in
1894 and then organised an international exhibition
in Liège the next year. In 1899 he opened a furniture
factory in Liège with a shop in Paris. Having
exhibited successfully in London and Paris, he
continued to develop his designs and his later
furniture foreshadows the art deco style.

Henry van de Velde (1863-1957) was the great
theoretician of Art Nouveau. Interested in all the
arts, he attended the Académie des Beaux Arts at
Antwerp, then he trained in Verlget's atelier, after
which he studied with Carolus Duran in Paris,
returning to Antwerp in 1886, when he co-founded

56

the circle Als ik Kan, and was involved in the foundation of L'Art Indépendent, an association of Neo-Impressionist painters, in 1887. Soon he joined Les XX, the avant-garde of the movement, and encountered the writings of Gauguin and Denis, the theories and principles of William Morris and the English Arts and Crafts Movement.

In the early 1890s van de Velde designed books and worked on the literary journal *Van Nu en Straks*, a beautifully produced and artistically very influential magazine published in Brussels and Antwerp from 1892 to 1901. The asymmetrical layout and virtually non-objective woodcuts were typographically and artistically revolutionary and extremely important for book design and illustration. At this time he left easel painting behind, and concentrated on the applied arts and architecture, in pursuance of his desire to create a complete and better environment by the application of rationalism in visible construction, logic in the use of materials, and a rejection of all nonfunctional ornament.

Van de Velde and Maria Sèthe, a member of Les XX, were married in 1894 and the next year built Bloemenwerf, which he designed, complete with all its contents including architectural fittings, wallpaper, furniture, carpets, china, glass and silver. It was a remarkable, imaginative and organic whole, which he extended by designing even his wife's dresses and jewellery. Visitors who were enchanted by the harmonious serenity of the house included Siegfried Bing, Julius Meier-Graefe, Count Harry Kessler and Karl-Ernst Osthaus, all of whom publicised van de Velde's work making it internationally known. The house embodies theories van de Velde had put forward in several publications: *Le Déblaiement d'Art* (1894), originally a lecture at Les XX, *L'Art futur* (1895) and *Aperçus en vue d'une synthèse d'art* (1895).

The furniture Bing asked van de Velde to design for his shop L'Art Nouveau in Paris was subsequently shown, with great success, in the international section of decorative arts at the Dresden exhibition in 1897. Julius Meier-Graefe asked van de Velde to design the interior of La Maison Moderne, his shop in Paris, and then introduced him to the avant-garde group in Berlin, where he moved in 1899, having received many commissions in Germany. He became the director of the Hohenzollern-Kunstgewerbehaus gallery in Berlin and redesigned the façade and interior fittings, designed the interior of the Folkwang Museum at Hagen and was the director of advertising and graphic design for the Tropon company of Mülheim. The poster illustrated is one of his most famous designs.

During the winter of 1900 to 1901, van de Velde went on a lecture tour in Germany, further publicising his theories. *Die Renaissance in Modernen Kunstge-werbe* was published in 1901, at the time when the Grand-Duke Wilhelm Ernst of Saxe-Weimar gave him the post of "conseiller artistique chargé de la mission de relever le niveau de la production des industries d'art de son pays" and he moved his family to Weimar. Van de Velde travelled to the Far East in 1903. In 1906 he supervised construction and became director of the Kunstgewerberschule in Weimar (which adjoined the Kunstschule), subsequently co-founding the Deutscher Werkbund, for which he designed the Werkbund Theatre of the 1914 Cologne exhibition. The Weimar Kunstgewerbeschule was the first in Europe to follow a systematic, prescribed study of styles, to repudiate the dependence on the past and to encourage imaginative but logical and sensible invention, and to regard the nature of the materials used as the most essential quality of any work of art. Van de Velde founded his doctrine on the triangle "Art, Perfection, Beauté".

As a Belgian, he had to resign all his posts at the outbreak of war and moved to Switzerland, as soon as it was allowed. Later he returned to Belgium, where he continued his distinguished career which subsequently included designing the Kröller-Müller Museum in Otterlo, founding and directing the Institut Supérieur des Arts Décoratifs at La Cambre, Brussels, teaching architecture at the University of Ghent but most of all writing the considerable, penetrating, influential body of work summarised in *Formules de la beauté architectonique moderne*.

Victor Horta (1861-1947) designed the Hôtel Tassel (1893) as an architectural manifesto. It was the first, and most complete, Art Nouveau house design which considerably influenced Guimard among others. Horta concentrated on architecture but some of his contemporaries worked in a number

T. van Rysselberghe: *La Libre Esthétique*, 1896, L of C

P. Livemont: *Absinthe Robette*, 1896, L of C

of different fields. These included Paul Cauchie (1875-1952), who designed wallpapers, furniture, tapestries, mosaics, posters and house interiors. Unlike Horta and van de Velde, the architect Paul Hankar (1859-1901) was more involved with the decorative elements of a building than with the interior spaces. Influenced particularly by Oriental art and by the historicism of Viollet-le-Duc, Hankar's designs were much appreciated by the Belgian artistic community.

Adolphe Crespin (1859-1944) designed one of

his finest posters for his friend Paul Hankar, with whom he collaborated on a number of buildings. Crespin trained at the Académie in Brussels, and studied with Bonnat in Paris and then travelled to France, Spain, Italy and England. In 1894 Crespin became professor of drawing at the Ecole d'Art in Schaerbeek and met Hankar then. One of his pupils was Henri Evenepoel (1872-1899) who moved to Paris from Brussels in 1892 and studied decorative painting before becoming a pupil of Gustave Moreau. Evenepoel first exhibited in 1894 with the Société

P. Livemont: *Cercle Artistique*, 1895, L of C

J. Ensor: *Salon des Cent*
1898, L of C

P. Livemont: *La
Réforme*,
1897, L of C

H. Meunier: *Rajah*,
1898, L of C

62

H. Meunier: *Casino de Blankenberghe*, 1896, L of C

A. Donnay: *[Régate]* c. 1895, L of C

des Artistes Français and then showed at the Salon of the Société Nationale des Beaux-Arts. After his untimely death, there was an exhibition of his works at the salon of La Libre Esthétique. Crespin also collaborated successfully with Edouard Duyck (1856-1897) on poster designs, theatre designs and decorations for a room in the Colonial exhibition at Tervueren; this was a section of the 1897 Brussels Exhibition which was held in a suburb of the city and was devoted to the Congo. Hankar, Serurrurier-Bovy and van de Velde were all involved in the pavilion designs.

Van de Velde's wife's brother-in-law Théo van Rysselberghe (1862-1926) was a prolific, influential artist who was one of the co-founders of Les XX. After studying at the Academies of Ghent and Brussels, he travelled in Spain and Morocco from 1882 to 1884. During a visit to Paris in 1888 he met Seurat and adopted a Neo-Impressionist technique. In the mid-1890s, under van de Velde's influence he turned to the decorative arts and designed book illustrations, furniture, jewellery, murals and posters, playing an important part in the revival of applied art in Belgium. From 1898 he spent much time in Paris, in Symbolist circles. Later he retired to Provence.

One of van de Velde's collaborators was Georges Lemmen (1865-1916) who designed the typeface for van de Velde's 1908 edition of *Also Sprach Zarathrustra* Lemmen exhibited annually with Les XX from 1889, and then with La Libre Esthétique, for which some of his most interesting posters were designed, and was one of the founders of L'Estampein 1906. He had trained at the Académie des Beaux-

Arts of Saint-Josse-ten-Noode (Brussels).

Privat Livemont (1861-1936) studied at the Ecole des Arts Décoratifs in the same district. Having won an academic prize he went to Paris where he worked as a decorator and theatre designer, and studied at the Ecole Etienne Marcel in the evenings. After six years he returned to Belgium, settled in Schaerbeek, and became a professor at the Académie. In 1890 his first poster won first prize in the *concours d'affiches* organised by the Cercle Artistique de Schaerbeek. Livemont's attractive, well-designed, meticulously executed posters were very successful and he received many commissions, including posters for *Absinthe Robette*, *Cacao Van Houten* and *Café Rajah*.

An earlier poster for *Café Rajah* was perhaps the most Art Nouveau design by Henri Meunier (1873-1922), who was the son of the engraver Jean-Baptiste Meunier and nephew of the sculptor Constantin Meunier. He was his father's pupil at the Académie in Brussels, after which he studied in Paris. From 1897 he exhibited with Le Sillon. After he returned to Belgium he became a professor at the Académie in Ixelles and also designed posters, theatre programmes, magazine illustrations and postcards. His designs are interesting not least because they presage the directness and simplicity of modern art.

Fernand Toussaint (1873-1955) also exhibited with Le Sillon, for whom he designed one of his few posters; during most of his long career as a genre and portrait painter, strongly influenced by the Symbolists, he exhibited in numerous exhibitions including La Libre Esthétique

The Symbolist painter Fernand Khnopff (1858-1921) studied at the Academy in Brussels and then in Paris, where he was particularly influenced by Moreau, Delacroix and the Pre-Raphaelites. In 1883 he was one of the co-founders of Les XX and exhibited at the first Salon de la Rose+Croix although his Belgian confrères discouraged this. He was eventually awarded the Order of Leopold for his services to painting, as was another co-founder of Les XX, James Ensor (1860-1949). Ensor was an innovative, imaginative artist whose work foreshadowed Expressionism. He executed paintings, drawings, pastels and etchings rather than graphics (although his poster for the Salon des Cent is interesting).

H. Obrist: *Embroidery* illustrations from *Pan*, 1895 L of C

P. Behrens: *Der Küss* illustrations from *Pan*, 1898

Félicien Rops (1833-1898) was a painter and etcher who was born in Namur and trained in Brussels but spent much of his life in Paris where he exhibited at the Salons although from 1886 to 1893 he was a member of Les XX. Rops' etchings were very successful; he taught Armand Rassenfosse (1862-1934) the techniques of engraving. Rassenfosse's only previous training had been lessons from a family friend. In about 1890 Rassenfosse encountered the publisher-printer Auguste Bénard which was the start of a long and successful working relationship; the posters are subtle, elegant and varied. Rassenfosse exhibited a great deal, at the Salon des Cent l'Art Indépendant, La Libre Esthétique and other salons. He designed many book illustrations and in 1898 Maurice Bauwens commissioned him to do the cover forLes Affichesétrangères illustrées. Maurice Siville founded the *Caprice Revue* with Rassenfosse, Auguste Donnay (1862-1921) and Emile Berchmans (1867-1947). Like the other two, Donnay was born in Liège; he trained at the Académie there before visiting Paris on a scholarship. In 1900 he was made Professor of Decorative Art at the Académie. In addition to working with Bénard, Donnay designed numerous illustrations for reviews and also exhibited regularly in Belgium and abroad, including with the Berlin Secession. Later in life he enjoyed success as a landscape painter. Emile Berchmans came from a family of artists and trained at the Académie in Liège. He worked on *La Plume* as well as on the *Caprice Revue* and the *Revue illustrée de Paris*. Moreover he designed many illustrations for books, calendars, magazines and printed ephemera. Well-known as a decorator, he showed at numerous exhibitions, including *La Libre Esthétique* and *L'Art Indépendant*. Rassenfosse, Donnay and Berchmans are three of the greatest Belgian poster artists.

E. Berchman: *Salon*
1896, L of C

Germany

During the reign of Wilhelm I Germany was unified under the Prussian crown; he became Emperor of Germany, largely thanks to his Iron Chancellor, Otto von Bismarck (1815-1898) and the efficient General Moltke. The duchies of Schleswig, Holstein and Lauenburg were annexed to Prussia in 1865 after the German-Danish war, and Prussia took control of several other German states, after her victory in the Seven Weeks War with Austria. At the end of the Franco-Prussian war, Alsace and Lorraine were acquired, France forced to pay an indemnity of five billion francs, and the German princes accepted the King of Prussia as their overlord. At Versailles in January 1871 he became the first Kaiser of the second Reich.

Wilhelm II succeeded in 1888, after his father's very brief reign, to an Empire which was the strongest power in continental Europe. After the Kaiser quarrelled with Bismarck for various reasons including Wilhelm's desire to make Germany a colonial power, various chancellors succeeded each other, the most effective of whom was Prince Chlodwig Hohenlohe-Schillingsfürst. Germany gradually alienated Great Britain as well as France and her old ally Russia, so that the balance of power was disturbed.

From 1870 until the First World War, Germany's population increased by about fifty per cent, much of it in the great urban industrial centres, notably the Ruhr conurbation; also there was considerable migration from the country to the cities. During this time Germany became a modern, powerful, industrial state, with strong feelings of national pride. The Kaiser's decision to build a powerful navy for the Empire underwrote rapid expansion of the steel industry, which surpassed that of Great Britain by 1910, as Germany's developing chemical, electrical and mechanical technologies had already done.

Agricultural production increased considerably with the use of modern methods, and foreign trade expanded greatly.

In Germany the Academies were as conservative as those elsewhere and numerous younger artists wished to be free of the historicist restrictions of the establishment. Die Elf (The XI) was formed in Berlin in 1892; members included Lovis Corinth (1858-1925), Max Klinger (1857-1910), Ludwig von Hoffmann (1861-1945), Max Liebermann (1847-1935) and Walter Leistikow (1865-1908). Some months later Munch exhibited, for the first time in Germany, at the Verein Berliner Künstler. There were objections to his work and the committee closed the exhibition, in spite of protests from a number of artists, who subsequently formed an association which later was to become the Berlin Secession. Before this Munich saw the founding of the Secession, in 1892, and the birth of the Jugendstil movement named for the magazine *Jugend* (Youth) which George Hirth founded in 1896 as Munich's answer to *Pan*. The satirical magazine *Simplicissimus* started the same year, and *Dekorative Kunst* the next.

The founders of the Munich Secession included Otto Eckmann (1865-1902), Thomas Theodor Heine (1867-1948), Max Liebermann (1847-1935), Franz Stuck (1863-1928), Lovis Corinth, Hans Thoma (1839-1924), Wilhelm Trübner (1851-1917), Peter Behrens (1868-1940) and Fritz von Uhde (1848-1911). Foreign members included Giovanni Segantini, Eugène Carrière (1849-1906) and Paul Besnard. The artistic styles of the founders varied very considerably, but Eckmann, Heine, Stuck and Behrens are permanently identified with the Jugendstil movement. Eckmann even auctioned all his paintings in order to devote himself wholeheartedly to the applied arts; both he and

67

Behrens were ultimately aiming for *Gesamtkunstwerk*, a total work of art.

Many of the Munich artists worked on the magazine *Pan* (the name means all in Greek), founded in Berlin in 1895 by Julius Meier-Graefe (1867-1935), the greatest critic of the time and an extremely influential figure in the history of l'Art Nouveau. Born in Hungary, the son of a German industrialist, Meier-Graefe went to Berlin in 1890 (after studying engineering in Munich and Zurich) where he moved in artistic circles, and began his writing career. During a visit to England in 1893 he met many of the leading artists of the time, including Beardsley, William Morris, Burne-Jones and others of his circle. Meier-Graefe was one of the founder-members of the Pan Association in Berlin and was one of the two first co-editors (with the poet Otto Julius Bierbaum) of the magazine. Beautifully produced and designed, innovative and original, *Pan* is a pleasure to read. There were disagreements and the two editors resigned after the third issue, although Meier-Graefe, in particular, had done much to launch the magazine. Subsequently he moved to Paris where he met Siegfried Bing. They travelled to Brussels together the same year where they met Henry van de Velde. Meier-Graefe introduced Bing to the work of the Jugendstil artists.

As early as 1896 Meier-Graefe was generally known as an "art critic". In 1897, he founded the magazine *Dekorative Kunst* in Munich; he wrote most of the first issue and continued to write many of the articles for the next three years. Bing wrote an important article for him on the future of design. Van de Velde designed the offices of the magazine and then, with Meier-Graefe, met many of the artistic avant-garde in Germany and decided to move there. Later on Meier-Graefe did some influential work for the magazine *Die Insel*, published in Berlin and Leipzig. Afterwards Meier-Graefe became disillusioned with the ideas of the 1890s and turned to writing history as well as art criticism and also travelled widely. Fleeing from Hitler's Germany, he became a French citizen at the end of his life.

Hermann Obrist's innovative exhibition of embroideries, executed by Bertha Ruchet, of April 1896 was discussed in the leading art periodicals, including *Pan*, as heralding the "birth of a new applied art". The exhibition travelled on from Munich to Berlin and London and was enthusiastically reviewed internationally. Obrist was born in Switzerland and, in 1887, after he left the university of Heidelburg, travelled in England and Scotland (his mother being Scottish), which stimulated his interest in the applied arts. After studying in Karlsruhe and at the Académie Julian in Paris, he moved to Berlin, then to Florence and, finally, to Munich. While the exhibition was on its travels, Obrist and several confrères founded the influential Vereinigte Werkstätten für Kunst im Handwerk, which still exists today.

The Vereinigte Werkstätten did not distinguish between machine and handmade production: the aim was to produce the best possible quality by whatever means. The designs, made by in-house or outside artists, approved by the board members, were made in the company's workshops and factories in Germany, not abroad, and then retailed in their own shops. This practical and pragmatic cooperation between artist, craftsman and manufacturer was soundly based in economic terms, nationalistic and extremely forward-thinking for its time: a precursor of the Deutscher Werkbund and the Bauhaus.

In order to publicise the new ideas Obrist gave many lectures and founded the Lehr-und Versuch-Ateliers für Angewandte und Freie Kunst with Wilhelm von Debschitz (1871-1948), a gifted and innovative teacher, to put his ideas into practice. The school was extremely successful. Its first student was Friedrich Adler (1878-1942?), who later taught at the school, and became an internationally distinguished designer of furniture, jewellery, metalwork, textiles and ivories.

Sadly, Obrist retired from the school in 1904, because his increasing deafness made teaching impractical, but through his writings, lectures, correspondence and discussions (for example with his friend Kandinsky) he extended his already considerable influence on both contemporary and later art. His designs approach abstraction as he used line, colour and form to express the dynamic of nature, aiming for an art which was an "intensification of life".

August Endell (1871-1925), born in Berlin, met

I. A. Rassenfosse: *The Improved Electric Glow Lamp*, 1895, L of C

his mentor, Obrist, early in 1896, after transferring to Munich from Tübingen university, and subsequently left academe for an artistic career. His brother, Fritz Endell (1873-1955) gave up theology for art under August's influence, and studied in Paris with Colarossi, specialising in wood-cuts. Later Fritz Endell moved to Stuttgart and then to the United States, but eventually returned to Germany.

August Endell designed furniture, lamps and stained-glass, as well as illustrations for various journals including *Pan*. In 1897, as one of the co-founders of the Vereinigte Werkstätten, his contribution to the first exhibition was a remarkable frieze which prefigures his designs for the Hof-Atelier Elvira, Munich (1897) where the extraordinary, swirling, anthropomorphic relief on the exterior was prophetically abstract. Endell's writings, including *Um die Schünheit* (1896), in which he clarified his theories and explained the psychology of perception, are very important in the history of twentieth-century art, not least because they were so influential for Kandinsky.

In 1901 he moved to Berlin, designing a number of buildings there including the Buntes Theatre (1901) and, later, several houses in which his style became more severe and functional. In 1904 Endell founded his own school, the Schule für Formkunst and, after the First World War, he became director of the Akademie für Kunst und Kunstgewerbe in Wroclaw.

Richard Riemerschmid (1868-1957) was a versatile artist, architect and designer who trained as a painter at the Munich Academy from 1888 to 1890. In 1897 he co-founded the Vereinigte Werkstätten and then concentrated on applied arts, after designing his own house in 1896. His brother-in-law, Karl Schmidt started the Werkstätte für Handwerkskunst in Dresden in 1898, where many Jugendstil designers worked. Later many German craft workshops joined forces under Schmidt's directions as the Deutsche Werkstätten and settled at Hellerau, near Dresden, where Riemerschmid planned the first low-cost garden city in Germany. Later he planned the garden city at Nürnberg.

Riemerschmid's interior designs were also very original; the Music Room for the Dresden Exhibition of 1899 and the Room of an Art Lover for the Paris

1900 Exposition were both much admired. In 1900 to 1901 he consolidated his reputation with the Munich Schauspielhaus, which is rightly regarded as one of Germany's most important Jugendstil buildings.

Moreover his designs for machine-made furniture which could be produced at a reasonable price in large quantities were very important in the history of applied arts in Germany. As a founder/member of the Deutscher Werkbund and as a teacher in Nürnberg, Munich (where he was head of the Kunstgewerbeschule) and Cologne (where he founded a Werkschule in 1926) he was one of the most influential industrial designers of the twentieth century.

One of the co-founders of the Munich Secession was Peter Behrens. Born in Hamburg, he moved to Munich in 1889 and studied with Hugo Kotschenreiter for three years, having previously studied in Karlsruhe from 1885 to 1887 and then in Düsseldorf for two years. The year after the Secession was founded, Behrens was one of the artists who started a group called the Freie Vereinigung Münchener Künstler. During the mid-1890s he

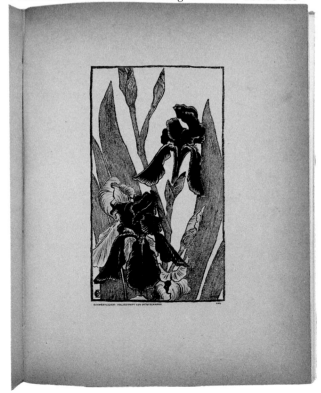

O. Eckmann: *Irises* illustration from, 1895, L of C

70

decided to give up painting and turned to applied arts. *The Kiss* is one of his magnificent woodcuts, commissioned by *Pan* and then illustrated in *Dekorative Kunst*. Behrens was one of the first to join the Vereinigte Werkstätten and was represented in the 1899 exhibition at the Glaspalast in Munich. That same year Grand Duke Ernst Ludwig of Hesse-Nassau invited him to join the artists' colony of Matildenhöhe in Darmstadt. At their first exhibition in 1901 Behrens showed his first architectural designs for his own house with all its furniture and fittings. At this time his style became more rectilinear and geometric, as is evident in his first typeface design, *Behrens-Fraktur* of 1902. In 1902 he encountered Mackintosh's designs at the Turin exhibition. In 1903, by Hermann Muthesius's arrangement, he became director of the Düsseldorf Kunstgewerbeschule which, under his reforming and innovative direction, became the leading design school in Germany. He moved on in 1907 to become artistic director for AEG in Berlin and designed appliances, typography, advertising and a number of

buildings including the pioneering turbine factory (1909). Behrens's assistants at this time included Le Corbusier, Walter Gropius and Mies van der Rohe.

From 1922 to 1936 Behrens was head of the Meisterschule für Architektur at the Akademie der Bildenden Künste in Vienna. In 1936 he became director of the Meister-atelier für Baukunst at the Prussian Academy of Arts in Berlin.

Otto Eckmann's woodcuts, especially *Irises* and *Three Swans on DarkWater*, made his reputation very quickly. He also designed vignettes and borders for *Pan* and covers and ornaments for *Jugend*. Eckmann was interested in Japanese prints, having studied Justus Brinckmann's collection in Hamburg. Born in Hamburg, Eckmann studied there, in Nürnberg and then at the Munich Academy after 1885. Although he was achieving success as a Symbolist painter, he auctioned all his pictures in 1894 and turned to applied arts, designing furniture, jewellery, stained-glass, metalwork and tapestries.

Beginning in 1896 Eckmann provided tapestry designs for the Kunstwebschule at Scherrebek in

F. Stuck: *VII Exposition Internationale de Beaux-Arts*, 1897, L of C

72

Berlin. Before his premature death from tuberculosis he designed numerous graphics, (some of which were commissioned by the forward-thinking Emil Rathenau, founder of AEG) wallpapers, carpets, tapestries and, after his highly-regarded titlepage for *Die Woche* (1900), the most famous of all Art Nouveau typefaces - *Eckmann-Schmuck*.

Another artist who hoped, like Eckmann, Behrens and Richard Riemerschmid, to achieve the *Gesamtkunstwerk*, was Franz von Stuck (1863-1928). Stuck was born in Lower Bavaria and studied at the Kunstgewerbeschule and then at the Academy in Munich for four years until 1885. A painter, illustrator, graphic artist, architect and gifted teacher, Stuck co-founded the Munich Secession with Bruno Piglheim, Fritz von Uhde and Heinrich von Zügel. In 1895 he was appointed professor at the Munich Academy and rapidly became one of the best known art teachers in Germany. Remarkably, his pupils included Wassily Kandinsky, Josef Albers

Schleswig (now Denmark) including *Five Swans*, one of his most famous. In 1897, an extraordinary year for him, his metalwork designs were first shown at the Glaspalast exhibtion in Munich; his book *Neue Formen. Dekorative Entwurfe für die Praxis* appeared to critical acclaim, and was very influential for other artists; he received a number of tapestry commissions; Grand Duke Ernst Ludwig of Hesse-Nassau asked him to design the study in his Neue Palais at Darmstadt; and he became instructor in ornamental painting at the Kunstgewerbeschule in

T. T. Heine: *Programm*
[Marya de Wardl] c. 1910
L of C

and Paul Klee.

In Munich during 1897 and 1898 Stuck designed his own house - and all its decoration, furniture and fittings - which was a true *Gesamtkunstwerk*, for which he deservedly won several awards. Also in 1897 Stuck produced the poster for the *VII. Internationale Kunstaustellung*, one of his most famous designs whose restrained colour palette and striking layout proved extremely influential for poster designers of the future.

Bruno Paul (1874-1968), after attending the Kunstgewerbeschule in Dresden, studied at the Academy in Munich while Stuck was teaching there. Paul drew a great many illustrations for *Jugend* and *Simplicissimus*. In 1897 he was a co-founder of the Vereinigte Werkstätten and was, in 1907, a co-founder of the Deutscher Werkbund. The same year he became director of the school attached to the Kunst-gewerbemuseum in Berlin and, when the school was combined with the Akademische

Caricatur von Th. Th. Heine

Hochschule für Bildende Künste in 1924, he became director of the Vereinigte Staatsschulen für Freie und Angewandte Kunst until he resigned in 1933 and moved to Düsseldorf. Paul's architectural designs were particularly admired by such contemporaries as Hermann Muthesius, the writer, but his designs for applied arts and his posters were also highly successful.

Stuck also influenced the work of Carl Strathmann (1866-1939) who studied in Düsseldorf, where he was born and then at the Kunstschule in Weimar. Strathmann moved to Munich and painted for some years in a style much influenced by Jan Toorop. In 1894 he became a member of the Munich Freie Vereinigung, a group which had split from the Secession, together with Behrens, Eckmann, Adalbert Niemeyer (1867-1932), his old friend Heine and others. Later in his career he produced graphic designs in an ornamental, convoluted style.

Thomas Theodor Heine (1867-1948) was born in

B. Paul: *Ausstellung*,
1906, L of C

73

H. Christiansen:

L'Heure from
du Berger illustration
L'Estampe Moderne,
L of C

L. Hohlwein:
Kunstgewerbehaus, 1908,
L of C

L. Hohlwein: *Winter in Bayern*, 1908, L of C

Leipzig and studied in Düsseldorf and then in Munchen, from 1885 to 1888. Apparently his father stopped his allowance in 1892 so he turned to his caricatures and illustrations for income, rather than painting full-time as he had done before. In 1896 Heine and Albert Langen, the publisher of *Fliegende Blätter*, co-founded *Simplicissimus*, a satirical illustrated weekly, which soon became a household word in Germany. Heine's uniquely acerbic, spare, striking designs were very successful, although they earned him a jail-term. He also designed illustrations for a number of books including Oscar Wilde's *Salome* and Thomas Mann's *Walsungenblut*. One of his most famous designs was a poster and programme for Die elf Scharfrichter, the German equivalent of the Chat Noir. Heine's striking designs were influential for a number of artists, including Ludwig Hohlwein (1874-1949) who was also influenced by the

Beggarstaff Brothers and became one of Germany's greatest poster designers. In 1933 *Simplicissimus* was banned by the Nazis and Heine fled to Prague, from there to Oslo and then to Sweden, where he continued to draw caricatures and to paint, for the rest of his career.

Angelo Jank (1868-1940) was born in Munich and studied at the Academy from 1891 to 1896. He became a member of Die Scholle, a group of artists, many of whom worked on *Jugend*, which included Leo Putz (1869-1940), later a member of the Munich and Berlin Secessions, and Walter Georgi (1871-1924). Albert Weisgerber (1878-1915) was a pupil of Stuck at the Academy and succeeded Jank as teacher of drawing at the Ladies' Academy in Munich. In 1913 he was a co-founder and first President of the Neue Secession in Munich. Weisgerber's designs for *Jugend* are Art Nouveau in style, with elegant lines,

A. Jank: *Ausstellung*,
1897 L of C

J.Witzel: *Deutsche Kunst und Dekoration*, 1896 , L of C

influenced by the year he spent in Paris in 1905 to 1906.

One of the most prolific contributors to *Jugend* was Julius Diez (1870-1954), nephew of Wilhelm Diez, the painter, who studied at the Munich Kunstgewerbeschule and then the Academy, having moved to Munich from Nürnberg, where he was born. From 1907 he was a professor at the Kunstgewerbeschule and from 1925 at the Academy, that same year he became president of the Secession. Diez continued to paint as well as design ceramics, glass, murals, typographics and a number of posters. His work and teaching influenced a whole generation of designers, including Eugène Cordier (1903-1974), Franz Paul Glass (1886- 1964), and Friedrich Heubner (1886-1974). Hans Christiansen

(1866-1945) was one of scores of artists who worked on *Jugend* but his importance lies more in his writings which incude *Neue Flachenornamente* (1892). Christiansen studied at the Kunstgewerbeschule in Hamburg and then established a Geschaft für Dekorationsmalerie there. While attending the Académie Julian in Paris from 1896 to 1899, he exhibited in the applied arts section of the Darmstadt 1898 exhibition which was organised by Alexander Koch (1860-1939), the publisher of *Zeitschrift für Innendekoration* (founded in 1889) and of *Deutsche Kunst und Dekoration* (founded in 1897 - the same year as *Kunst und Dekoration*). Christiansen was invited by the Grand Duke Ludwig Ernst of Hesse in 1898 to move to Darmstadt and found an artists' colony there.

M. H. Baille Scott: *Haus Eines Kunst-Freundes*, 1902, L of C

J. Diez: Munchen, 1908,
L of C

Situated on Matildenhöhe, the colony was officially inaugurated in 1899: the participants were Christiansen, Paul Burck (1878-1947), Patriz Hüber (1878-1902), Ludwig Habich (1872-1949), Rudolf Bosselt (1871-1938) and Heinrich Vogder (1872-1942) who drew many illustrations for *Die Insel* in a style influenced by Beardsley. They were soon joined by Olbrich and Behrens. In 1901 the colony held a large exhibition entitled *Ein Dokument Deutsche Kunst*, which was fairly successful critically but not financially. It was, nevertheless, architecturally a magnificent achievement.

In December 1901 Alexander Koch, through his magazine *Zeitschrift für Innendekoration* held a competition for the *Haus Eines Kunstfreundes* (including interiors) which was won by Mackay Hugh Ballie Scott (1895-1945). Charles Rennie Mackintosh's masterly and influential designs took second place. The three winning designs were published in 1902, with a preface by Hermann Muthesius (1861-1927), an attaché at the German Embassy in London and later author of *Das Englische Haus* (1905), a very interesting book about contemporary British architecture.

In his quest for the best industrial design, Herman Muthesius collected a group of artists, industrialists, and designers who together established the Deutscher Werkbund on October 6, 1907 the designers included Reimerschmid, Behrens, Olbrich, van de Velde, Paul, Pankok, Schmidt, Fischer, Hoffmann, Poelzig and Tessenow. In 1914 a great debate between van de Velde and Muthesius took place with Muthesius speaking for machine production and van de Velde speaking for individual artistic creation.

The Werkbund theatre, designed by Obrist and van de Velde, was one of the last buildings of Art Nouveau; the model factory by Adolf Meyer and Walter Gropius (van de Velde's succcessor at Weimar) presaged the future.

J. Gipkens: *Deutsche Austellung*, 191-, L of C

Austria-Hungary

In 1910 the Empire consisted of Austria, Hungary, Bohemia-Moravia, Croatia, Galicia and Bosnia, the last having been annexed in 1908 by the Austrians much against the wishes of the Serbs and the Russians. This chapter roughly covers present-day Austria, Czechoslovakia and Hungary; Poland is discussed in a separate section.

In the Compromise of 1867 the Emperor Franz Joseph surrendered many of his prerogatives within Hungary in exchange for Hungary's guaranteed support in foreign affairs and in time of war. The state was known as Austria-Hungary and the rest of the Imperial lands, which had no homogeneity but that they were Hapsburg possessions, were simply referred to as 'the kingdoms and lands represented in the Reichsrat'.

Eduard, Graf von Taafe became Kaiserminister in 1879 and for the next twelve years he succeeded in keeping the complicated political situation in balance, aided by Gustaf, Graf Kalnoky, the able foreign minister who recovered much of Austria's international prestige. Taafe finally resigned over the issue of universal suffrage, which Beck eventually carried through the Reichsrat in 1906. In the meantime Kasimir, Graf Badeni, took office in 1895 and, in his endeavour to settle the conflict between the Czechs and the Germans which was one of many constant problems within the empire, he promulgated an ordinance which put Czechs and Germans on an equal basis within Bohemia; there were so many German demonstrations, however, that the Emperor was alarmed and dismissed Badeni.

As well as the suffrage bill, Freiherr von Beck reached a fair compromise with Hungary on tariffs and made a number of reforms, but he left office as a result of the Bosnian crisis in which he opposed the views of Aloys von Aehrenthal, the foreign minister.

In 1908 Austria annexed Bosnia and Herzegovina, two Turkish provinces she had occupied since 1878. The outraged Serbs appealed to the Russians who protested to both Austria and Germany but, because they were recovering from the Russo-Japanese War and the 1905 revolution, were unable to back up their protests. The aggressive Aehrenthal, seeing little to be gained, declined to go to war with Serbia

K. Moser: cover for *Ver Sacrum*, 1899, Brighton

84

W. Jonsach: *Textile design [postcard]*, c. 1912, Va.

alone.

Later, after the Balkan Wars, Albania came into being, partly because the Austrians were determined that the area should not become Serbian. In June 1914, Archduke Franz Ferdinand, the Emperor's heir, was assassinated in Sarajevo. Discovering that the assassination had been planned in Belgrade, the

Austrians sent a provocative ultimatum to Serbia, rejected the Serbs' answer and declared war. The First World War ensued.

During the Emperor's long reign Vienna grew from an essentially medieval city to a modern, prosperous capital. The city's population quadrupled, there was much rebuilding, the Ringstrasse was constructed around the old city, the river Wien was vaulted, a tram system was installed and the metropolitan railway built. As the hub of a vast empire, Vienna was a magnet for people from all the provinces and therefore a cosmopolitan, lively city albeit weighed down by the dead hand of bureaucracy, and conscious of the darker side of life which obtruded at times as in 1889 with the scandal of the death of the Crown Prince and in 1898 when the Empress Elizabeth was assassinated. This was the time called *Gründerjahre* (years of reckless financial speculation) when fortunes were made and lost

K. Moser: *Illustrierte Zeitung*, 1900, L of C

E. Heckel & E. L. Kirchner: *Der neue Kunstsalon*, 1912?, L of C

1942), he had carried out decorative schemes in several theatres, including the Burgtheater, and in the Kunsthistorisches Museum from 1890 to 1892 when his brother died. In 1893 the Ministry of Culture, inexplicably, had refused to confirm Klimt's appointment as Professor at the Academy of Fine Arts. During the next few years Klimt painted few pictures, but each one is important to the development of his art, and one can trace his interest in Japanese art, contemporary French painting, pre-classical Greek art, the Munich Secession, Jan Toorop's work and Symbolism.

In the spring of 1897 many members of the Kunstlerhaus resigned, in protest against the conservative selection policy of the committee among other things, and formed the Secession (which was to be primarily an exhibition society) on April 3. About a year later *Ver Sacrum* started publication and the first exhibition, including works by a number of foreign artists, opened, at the

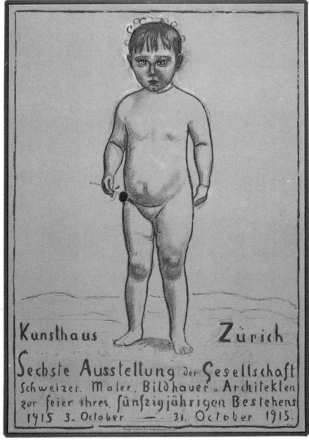

overnight, when the bourgeoisie spent money on new art and architecture and when Vienna led the world in both art and science.

A Christian-Socialist, Dr. Karl Lueger was appointed Mayor of Vienna in 1897; this was a remarkable alteration in Viennese politics which was, at first, opposed by the Emperor, who disliked Lueger. The same year the Vienna Secession (Vereinigung bildender Künstler Osterreichs Sezession) was set up. The group exhibited annually and published the magazine *Ver Sacrum* (Sacred Spring) which was beautifully produced, a *Gesamtkunstwerk* in itself, with unified typography, illustrations and design.

One of the co-founders and the first President of the Secession was Gustav Klimt (1862-1918). As a student at the Kunstgewerbeschule in Vienna, Klimt was influenced by the English Pre-Raphaelites and by the history painter Hans Makart (1840-1884). With his brother Ernst and Franz von Matsch (1861-

F. Hodler: *Kunsthaus*, Zurich, 1915, L of C

J. M. Olbrich:*Kölner
Ausstellung*, 190-, L of C

Horticultural Society's Hall, to an enthusiastic response by the public and even a visit from the Emperor, who was welcomed by the elderly honorary president, Rudolf von Alt, the watercolour artist. The exhibition poster and programme cover were designed by Klimt.The architect Josef Olbrich (1867-1908) designed the Secession Building, incorporating some preliminary sketches by Klimt into his design. It is a remarkable building with Moorish overtones, dominated by its foliated golden dome. The art critic Ludwig Hevesi composed the inscription over the entrance *Der Zeit ihre Kunst, der Kunst ihre Freiheit* (To the Age its Art, to Art its Freedom).

At the second exhibition Klimt showed Pallas Athena, with an integral frame executed by his brother Georg, and *Schubert at the Piano*, a painting commissioned for the music room of Nikolaus von

J. M. Olbrich:
Darmstadt,
1901, L of C

Dumba's large house on the Ringstrasse. Dumba was one of several generous patrons of the Secession that included the textile magnate Fritz Wärndorfer, the steel king Karl Wittgenstein, the Knips and Lederer families, for whom Klimt painted the Whistler-influenced, shimmeringly beautiful portrait of Serena Lederer (1899).

For several years Klimt then concentrated on three large murals for the ceiling of the Great Hall of the University of Vienna, representing *Philosophy, Medicine and Jurisprudence*; the complex, innovative, avant-garde paintings were eventually rejected by the University, after tremendous controversy, although *Philosophy* won a gold medal at the 1900 Paris Exposition.

In 1901 the Secessionists decided to devote an

A. Mucha: *Gismonda*,
1894/5, BN

exhibition to the *Gesamtkunstwerk*, built around a sculpture of Beethoven by Max Klinger and a frieze by Klimt which expressed the ideas of the Ninth Symphony, Schiller's *Ode to Jot*. The frieze owes a debt to the work of the great Swiss painter Ferdinand Hodler (1853-1918) who also admired Klimt. Hodler studied in Geneva and then travelled widely, eventually settling in Munich. His work was influenced by the Pre-Raphaelites whose work he first encountered with the Nabis in Paris, and by Puvis de Chavannes, whose calm monumentality and cool colours are reflected in Hodler's work from the 1890s on. From 1900 he belonged to the Berlin Secession and in 1904 he exhibited at the Vienna Secession, with considerable success.

In 1903 Klimt visited Italy twice and was enchanted by the Ravenna mosaics; he began painting in his "golden style" as exemplified by *Dana* and *Portrait of Adele Bloch-Bauer*. At this time he was painting a number of landscapes which are powerful evocations of nature, some of which were shown in his major retrospective exhibition at the Secession.

This eighteenth exhibition in 1903 was the artistic highpoint of the early years of the Secession but there was a growing rift developing, exacerbated by the débâcle over the St. Louis exhibition of 1904. The split was between the *Klimtgruppe* which included Wagner, Hoffmann, Moser and Moll and the *Nur-Maler* (pure painters), led by Engelhart, who espoused an insipid version of Impressionism.

Joseph Hoffman and the Weiner Werkstätte were asked by Alphonse Stoclet, a Belgian steel magnate, and his wife Suzanne, to design and build their house in Brussels. Klimt was asked to design three marble mosaics for the walls of the dining-room: on each of the two long walls a Tree of Life and on a short wall, a mandala. These mosaics were Klimt's last great mural scheme, influenced by the mosaics he had seen in Ravenna and by the Stoclets' Oriental art collection.

Klimt was successful in the exhibitions of 1908 and 1909, held at the Kunstchau (a temporary pavilion built by Josef Hoffmann), particularly with his glittering, golden painting *Der Kus* (1907-8), showing an embracing couple, one of Klimt's leitmotifs, which was bought by the government. In the autumn of 1909 he went to Paris and was

extremely impressed by the work of Toulouse-Lautrec and the Fauves. Clearly he was also affected by the work of Oskar Kokoschka (1886-1980) and Egon Schiele (1890-1918), whom he influenced previously. Continuing to paint portraits, he produced several dramatic allegories including *The Virgin* (1913) and *The Bride* (un-finished). A great draughtsman, designer and painter, he was one of the artistic geniuses of his time. The great architect Otto Wagner (1841-1918) first designed in a Renaissance-inspired style but moved on to a simple, geometrical, functional but spatially-complex style which he set forth in his book *Moderne Architektur* which was extremely influential on the younger generation in Austria and in Italy. Two of Wagner's pupils, famous in their own right, were also members of the Secession; Josef Hoffmann (1870-1956) and Joseph Maria Olbrich (1867-1908).

Olbrich was born in Troppau, the capital of the Austrian Duchy of Silesia, now Opava, Czechoslovakia and, at fourteen, enrolled in the building department of the Staatsgewerbeschule in Vienna. Encouraged by Camillo Sitte, the Director, he went on to the Spezialschule für Architektur, Akademie der Schonen Künstel in 1890 where he was taught by Baron Carl von Hasenauer, among others. Olbrich was a very successful student and eventually won the Prix de Rome; his travels were interrupted by some time spent working in Wagner's office but he visited Italy, Tunisia, Germany, France and England. In 1894 he was accepted as a member of the Künstlerhaus, and in 1897 he was one of thirteen members who resigned, including the nine original members of the Secession who were: Klimt, Ernst Stöhr (1860-1917), Johann Viktor Krämer, Moser, Moll, Rudolf Bacher (1862-1945), Julius Mayreder, Hoffmann and Olbrich.

Olbrich designed the entrance and main exhibition rooms of the Secession I exhibition, which were admired. In 1898 the Secession Building was completed in time for the Secession II exhibition. One of Olbrich's most successful and visionary buildings, the Secession Haus led to a number of other commissions. One of the most exciting was the invitation from the Grand Duke Ernst Ludwig of Hesse to design an artists' colony in his capital of Darmstadt. Olbrich's poster for the

A. Mucha: *La Tosca*, 1899, BN

J. Klinger: *Ausstellung,*
1909, L of C

exhibition *Ein Dokument Deutscher Kunst* of 1901 is based on the facade of the Ernst Ludwig Haus. Olbrich spent eight years in Darmstadt and the Wedding Tower and Colony buildings, with the Secession Haus and the Warenhaus Tietz in Düsseldorf, are probably his finest and best-known buildings. Olbrich's untimely death from leukaemia was recognised internationally as a great loss to art and architecture.

Hoffmann was born in Moravia and studied architecture at the Academy in Vienna for three years, graduating in 1895, having won the Prix de Rome. After a year's study in Italy and Dalmatia, he returned to Vienna and worked with Wagner. In 1899 he was appointed professor at the Kunstgewer-beschule. In 1903, with Kolo Moser and Fritz Wärndorfer, who became the financial director, he founded the Wiener Werkstätte. Their first two major commissions were the Purkersdorf Sanatorium (1904-8) and the Palais Stoclet, Brussels. Many of his pupils went on to work at the Wiener Werkstätte, including Wilhelm Jonasch (1892-?), a textile and graphic designer. Hoffmann's style changed over the years from a curvilinear, French-inspired form of Art Nouveau to one more geometric, influenced by Charles Rennie Mackintosh and the English Arts and Crafts movement. Later his style became more elegant and refined, presaging Art Deco.

The other artistic founder of the Wiener Werkstätte was Koloman Moser (1868-1918), painter and graphic artist. Moser was born in Vienna and entered the Akademie when he was seventeen, moving on to the Kunstgewerbeschule in 1892. In 1895 Moser met Julius Klinger (1876-1950), in the workshops of the Wiener Mode designers, and introduced him to the *Meggendorfer Blätte*. Klinger went on to work for a number of magazines in

A. Mucha: *Femme à la Marguerite*, c. 1900, BN

Vienna, Munich and Berlin where he lived from 1897 to 1915, and enjoyed considerable success particularly with his posters as well as his own books on ornament. After the First World War he opened an atelier in Vienna, having quarrelled with the Wiener Werkstätte.

Through the publisher Martin Gerlach, Moser met Klimt in 1895 and became one of the founder members of the Siebener Club of young artists which eventually, with others, became the Secession. Another group called the Hagengesellschaft (named after the landlord of the inn where they ate) seceded from the Künstlerhaus in 1900 and founded the Künstlerbund Hagen (the Hagenbund), holding their first exhibition in their own building in 1902. Moser designed posters and catalogue covers for the Secession, as well as designing many illustrations for Ver Sacrum. In 1899 he became an instructor at the

Kunstgewerbeschule and, the next year, a professor. Moser designed graphics, stained-glass windows, embroideries. As a result of the splendid eighth Secession exhibition in which Mackintosh and the other Glasgow artists, Henry van de Velde and C. R. Ashbee showed work, Moser's style became more geometric and rectilinear.

In 1901 Moser began designing for the theatre, but returned to stained-glass designs for the XIV Secession Exhibition of 1902. The next year the Wiener Werkstätte started and went on from strength to strength artistically. In 1907 a theatre and cabaret Die Fledermaus was opened by Fritz Wärndorfer. Hoffmann designed the fittings and decoration supplied by the Wiener Werkstätte and a number of artists designed the posters and programme covers. Moser also worked for various periodicals and was commissioned to design the

Mannheim. At the same time he designed for several plays and musical shows. Versatile, gifted, innovative, his importance lies not only in his work but also in his influence on the next generation.

Moser used the very Viennese *quadratl* style, derived from the work of the Glasgow School and Dutch graphic designers, for many of his illustrations for *Ver Sacrum*, as did several other designers including Hoffmann and Alfred Roller (1864-1935). An early member of the Secession, Roller designed the cover for the first number of *Ver Sacrum* and was head of the editorial committee for some time. In 1899 he was appointed professor at the Kunstgewerbeschule, and later married one of his students, Mileva Stoisavljevic. An extremely gifted draughtsman, Roller designed numerous illustrations for *Ver Sacrum*, posters and catalogue covers for the Secession, murals and mosaics. Much of his career was spent, however, as a theatre designer, presaged

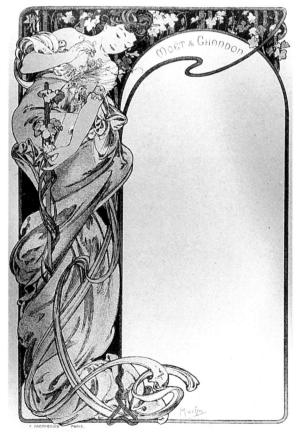

A. Mucha: *La Rose*, 1897, Va.

A. Mucha: *Moet et Chandon* [advertisment postcard], 1899, Va.

official souvenir book of the Emperor's Jubilee in 1904. Subsequently he was asked to design postage stamps for Bosnia and then for Austria.

In 1907 Moser changed direction to spend more of his time painting and held his first solo exhibition at the Miethke Gallery in Vienna in 1912, followed by shows in Budapest, Rome, Düsseldorf and

by his brilliant exhibition designs for the Secession. At the opening of the fourteenth (Beethoven) exhibition, Carl Moll (1861-1945) introduced Roller and Gustav Mahler, which proved to be the start of a long and fruitful working relationship. Eventually Roller left the Kunstgewerbeschule and became head of design at the Imperial Opera, returning to the Kunstgewerbeschule as Director in 1909. Elected to the committee of the Deutscher Werkbund, he joined the Osterreichischer Werkbund inaugurated in 1912.

Karl Otto Czeschka (1878-1960) also taught at the Kunstgewerbeschule for some years, moving on as Professor at the Kunstgewerbeschule in Hamburg from 1907 to 1943. Czeschka joined the Secession in 1900 and designed for the Wiener Werkstätte from 1905, continuing to contribute after his move to Hamburg. Czeschka designed fabrics, embroideries, interiors, furniture, stained-glass windows, calendars, magazine illustrations, commercial graphics and

A. Mucha: *Monaco.*
Monte Carlo, 1897, BN

A. Mucha: *Salon des Cent*, 1897, BN

theatre sets and costumes, for Max Reinhardt, the cabaret Fledermaus and the Hamburg Lessing-Gesellschaft. Gifted and versatile, probably Czeschka's most important commission was for book designs and illustrations for Verlag Gerlach of Vienna, in which his organisation of space, sparing use of colour and striking silhouette forms have a remarkably modern look.

Bertold Löffler (1874-1960) took over from Czeschka at the Kunstgewerbeschule in Vienna and continued to teach there until 1935. He was born in Bohemia and attended drawing school in Reichenberg, before studying at the Vienna Kunstgewerbeschule. In 1906 he founded the Wiener Keramik with Michael Powolny (one of the Hagenbund) and the company successfully sold through the Wiener Werkstätte for some years. Löffler also painted, the frescoes in the Salzburg Volkskeller (1913), for example, but most of his oeuvre was graphic designs of all sorts; illustrations

93

A. Mucha: *Société Populaire des Beaux-Arts*, 1897, BN

of folklore and legend was matched by artisic interest in folk art and ornament. There was also great interest evinced in Oriental art.

One of Hungary's best-known painter-designers, József Rippl-Rónai (1867-1927) studied in Vienna, Munich and Paris where he became friendly with the Nabis - Denis' influence is clear in his work. Rippl-Rónai travelled within France during his years there, including a visit to Pont-Aven, and came to know many artists. In 1901 he visited Holland and Russia, and then returned to Hungary.

János Vaszary (1867-1939), like Rippl-Rónai, appreciated Puvis de Chavannes, whose work he had admired while studying in Paris. Vaszary's painting style evolved to Expressionism, probably influenced by his studies in Munich, but his graphic designs were witty, linear and attractive.

József Divéky (1887-1951), one of the most prolific artists of the younger generation, after studying in Vienna, worked in Zürich and Brussels for the publishers Brüder Rosenbaum and then settled in Switzerland in 1919. In 1941 he was appointed Professor at the Budapest Arts and Crafts School. Divéky's powerful graphic style is more detailed then that of Elek Falus (1884-1950) who settled at Nagybánya and later in Munich, eventually working in Kecskemét. Falus' graphic designs were popular and influential including his work for *Nyugat* and the publishers Edition Nyguat.

Géza Faragó (1877-1928) studied in Paris and later worked at the artists' colony at Kecskemét. A graphic and theatre designer and painter, his attractive work is suited to its purpose, as are the designs of Sándor Nagy (1868-1950) who, after studying in Budapest, Rome and Paris, returned to Hungary and co-founded the artists colony at Gödölló, where he worked as a designer, painter and illustrator.

Mihály Biró (1886-1948) was best known as a poster designer. While his early graphics in Art Noueau style are attractive and interesting, his latter posters are realist and very powerful. He studied first in Budapest, and then in Berlin, Paris and London, winning a poster competition held by *The Studio* in 1910. After he returned to Hungary, his Socialist propaganda posters were so succesful that eventually he had to flee the country, not returning home until

for books and periodicals, posters, ex libris, commercial art, postcards, postage stamps and banknotes.

Adolf Loos (1870-1933) was born in Brno, the capital of Moravia, and trained as a mason before studying from 1890 to 1893 at the Technischen Hochschule Dresden, after which he spent three years in America. In Vienna he worked for a time as Carl Mayreder's assistant and briefly joined the Secession. Loos began writing in 1897 and published *Ornamentlosigkeit* in 1908. He was a member of Karl Kraus's circle which included Arnold Schoenberg, George Trakl the poet, and Oskar Kokoschka, whom Loos helped and assisted in every way. Loos was a brilliant architect and a perceptive, powerful critic.

The social, economic and industrial expansion of Hungary was reflected in the growth of the towns and cities, especially Budapest. This situation was paralleled by the literary renaissance of the time, which is exemplified by the influential literary periodical *Nyugat* (The West). The literary revival

after the Second World War.

After studying in Budapest, Vienna, Berlin and Paris, Imre Földes (1881-?) returned to Hungary where he directed an independant institute of graphic art, at the same time designing numerous posters and illustrations in a very decorative, attractive style. In 1921 he moved to Timisoara to direct an institute there, and in 1935 to Bucharest.

William Andrew (Willy) Pogány (1882-1955) travelled in the other direction in that he also studied in Budapest, Munich and Paris, but then decided to travel to America, after a short visit to London where, however, he found such success as a book illustrator that he stayed for ten years. Much of his best work was done for George Harrap, who was also Harry Clarke's publisher. Pogány went to America in 1915 and lived in New York, apart from spending several years in California during the 1930s. In America, he illustrated books, painted murals, designed for the stage and worked for Warner Studios in Hollywood. Pogány fantastic, delicate and attractive style cont-inued in demand even after the Art Deco style had become popular

Frantisek Kupka (1871-1957) was one of many artists who gravitated to Vienna from all parts of the Empire. Born in Opacno, he graduated from the Academy of Fine Arts in Prague in 1892, where he was much influenced by the work of the Nazarenes, Josef Mánes (1820-1871), and his follower Mikulás Ales, and then he studied at the Academy in Vienna. The Kunstverein commissioned *Heine's Death Dream* which was much admired by the Empress at the exhibition so Kupka became an overnight success and received many commissions. Two years later he left Vienna for Paris, where he knew Mucha. After a visit to London, he studied at the Académie Julian. Kupka was always interested in Czech folk art; in France he studied Breton Celtic art, Islamic art and Greek vases, but he was constantly interested by the Vienerstil. From 1899 he worked as a spiritualist and as an illustrator for *La Plume*, *Cocorico* and other magazines and designed book illustrations including the *Song of Songs* and *Lysistrata*. Kupka's *Amorpha*, *Fugue in Two Colours* (1911/2) is one of the first intentionally non-representational pictures in Western art.

Several Czech artists visited Paris in the 1890s but

A. Mucha: *Sarah Bernhardt*, 1905/6, L of C

95

A. Mucha: *L'Année qui Vient* [calendar], 1897, BN

the Czech Secession had started with the Jubilee Exhibition of 1891. Mánes was the ideal of the younger generation, who were also influenced by the work of the Polish painter Jan Matejko. Josef Vachal's (1884-?) work is reminiscent of Toorop's figures with flowing hair. Frantisek Bilek (1872-1941) and Vojtech Preissig (1873-1944) were influenced by the Nazarenes. Jan Preisler (1872-1918), who taught at the Academy in Prague, was a co-founder of the Mánes group, who published the art review *Volne Smery*. Emil Orlik (1870-1932) was born in Prague, studied in Munich and worked in Vienna and Berlin. His travels included two visits to Japan as can be seen in his work.

One of the most popular and best known Czech Art Nouveau graphic artists was Alphonse Mucha. Born in Ivancice, Moravia (now part of Czechoslovakia) he started work in a scenepainting workshop in Vienna. While travelling one summer, he encountered Count Karl Khuen-Belasi who commissioned him to paint murals in his castle. Through the Count, Mucha met Wilhelm Kray, professor at the Munich Academy, where he studied successfully for two years, supported by the Count, taught by Johann Caspar Herterich and Ludwig von Lofftz and much influenced by the decorative painter Hans Makart. In 1888 Mucha went to Paris to study at the Académie Julian and subsequently the Académie Clarossi. After the Count's suicide in 1889, he had to earn his own living.

The publisher Armand Colin commissioned illustrations for a number of books, including the enchanting *Mémoires d'un Eléphant Blanc* of 1894. The illustrations for Xavier Marmier's *Les Contes des Grand-mères* of 1892 earned an Honourable Mention at the Salon. In the same year Mucha designed his first poster, after being commissioned to design postage stamps, menus, and journal illustrations.

In 1894 Mucha happened to be in the right place at the right time and shot to instant fame as a result. On Christmas Eve, he was correcting proofs for a friend at Lemercier's printing works when Sarah Bernhardt telephoned to say that she did not like the poster designed for her new production *Gismonda* (by Victorien Sardou) which was to be ready for billing on New Year's Day. As he was the only artist

available, Mucha was offered the job. His poster delighted Bernhardt and is one of Mucha's finest designs. From the moment it appeared on the streets of Paris it became a collector's item and Mucha became famous overnight. Bernhardt's business acumen and shrewd sense of publicity also aided Mucha and his career.

Gismonda was distinctively tall and narrow for the time and the overall scheme was very different from current designs by Chéret and others. In any case it was only a few years since colour posters had first appeared in Paris. Iconographically Bernhardt is shown as a symbol of Tragedy rather than as a great actress portraying a tragic heroine. The mosaics, the arch and the gown give the poster a Byzantine splendour, partially derived from Mucha's Slavic background, and different from most contemporary designs, although Grasset's posters, including his *Jeanne d'Arc* for Bernhardt, must have had some influence on Mucha. The colours are subdued but the colour contrasts make the figure stand out and the distinctive lettering is legible from a distance, although details like the bird in the spandrel are better viewed from close at hand. Sarah Bernhardt was so enthusiastic about this poster that she gave him a six-year contract; he designed eight posters for her after *Gismonda : La Dame aux Camélias*, for a play they produced together in 1896, *Lorenzaccio, La Samaritaine, Médée* (1898), *Hamlet,* and Sardou's *La Tosca* of 1899 (the play on which Puccini based the opera)*Theodora* (1899) and *l'Aiglon* (1900). He also designed sets, costumes, jewellery and printed ephemera for Bernhardt.

Over the next few years as Mucha's reputation grew he received prestigious commissions like some of the illustrations for the eminent historian Charles Seignobos *Scènes et èpisodes de l'histoire d'Allemagne* published in 1896-8. Commercial success brought numerous commissions and Mucha agreed to contract his lithographic work to the printer Champenois exclusively in return for a fixed (and generous) salary. Champenois suggested printing Mucha's designs as *panneaux decoratifs*, essentially posters without lettering, which were printed on silk, repp, velvet or special paper and sold for framing and display in houses or shops. The various delightful lithographic designs were reprinted by the astute

Champenois as posters, calendars, menus, postcards. *Les Quatre Saisons* of 1896 and *Les Fleurs* of 1897 are among the most attractive.

In June 1897 there was a Salon des Cent one-man exhibition of Mucha's oeuvre and *La Plume* devoted a special issue to his work. Some of the exhibits later travelled to Prague, Munich, Brussels, London and New York. Mucha designed several of his most famous posters at this time, including *Job, Monaco. Monte-Carlo* (1897), and *Waverley Cycles* (1899).

The most successful of Mucha's book illustrations are perhaps those for Robert de Flers' *Ilsée, Princesse de Tripoli*. The book is illustrated page by page and shows the influence both of Grasset's *Histoire des quatre fils Aymon* and of the work of Carlos Schwabe. Schwabe's book illustrations, especially for Baud-elaire's *Les Fleurs du Mal* of 1900, include some wonderful Art Nouveau floral ornaments. The work of Paul Ruty perhaps was influential too, especially his ornaments for *Mèmoires d'un Eléphant Blanc*. The illustrations for Ilsée are homogeneous; Byzantine in style, demonstrating Mucha's interest in Symbolism, influenced by Czech folk art (which the artist himself always said was the main source for le *style Mucha*) and typical of his Art Nouveau work. The book is a completely integrated work of art.

Of all Mucha's book illustrations, however, he regarded those for *Le Pater* (1899), for which he also wrote the commentary, as much the most important. The book is a statement of his religious, artistic and philosophical beliefs, and combines Symbolist, Masonic and religious ideas.

For some years after 1904 Mucha spent part of each year in America. The most interesting graphic work of this time was the series of *Beatitudes* done as a Christmas colour supplement to the Everybody's *Magazine* for December 1906. In these countrified illustrations with their stylised flower borders his devotion to the Slav cause is foreshadowed. In 1910 Mucha returned to settle in Czechoslovakia, executing a series of large paintings of the Slav epic from 1909 to 1928. He continued to work as a graphic designer until he died in 1939, soon after being questioned by the Gestapo.

Poland

After the Congress of Vienna in 1815, Poland was divided into several parts: Great Poland, with Poznan as its centre, was left to Prussia, Austria kept most of Galicia, the eastern borderlands were given to Russia and central Poland was made into the "Congress Kingdom" with the Emperor of Russia as its ruler. Several risings there were suppressed with severity.

During the 1860s the general policy of Russification was intensified, making use of the educational system (although secret patriotic instruction throughout the region kept Polish cultural traditions alive). To encourage Russification the government lowered customs barriers and transport tariffs between Russia and Congress Poland, which resulted in Polish industrial expansion. The coal and iron centre at Dabrowa Gornicza and the textile factories at Lodz became the main industrial region under Russian control and were protected against competition from the West. The Poles, excluded from the civil service and the government, turned to other endeavours. Agrarian reforms, which were much more generous to Polish peasants than Russian ones had been, resulted in considerable migration to the expanding towns. Commerce, industry and banking all developed apace. Townsmen were largely socialist and there grew up a large body in sympathy with the Russian social democratic movement.

After the Russian revolution of 1905, the Poles' dreams of independence seemed possible for a time but concessions made by Russia soon faded away.

Roman Dmowski led the National Democratic party which wanted to unite all Poles, with autonomy, within the Russian empire. The revolutionaries and nationalists, led by Jozef Pilsudski, wanted an independent Poland. After the first World War, this became a reality and Poland was re-born.

Prussian Poland fared reasonably well during the first fifteen years after the Congress of Vienna but then the government appointed a German *oberpräsident* who began to Germanise the country, including the educational system. After the revolution of 1848 the Germanisation programme, which had been modified, was reintensified by Bismarck. The whole population was unified in its dislike of Germany without the class differences evident elsewhere in Poland.

The little Republic of Krakow established by the Congress of Vienna survived well for about thirty years but in 1846 was occupied by Austria. The pretext was a revolt among Poles in Galicia. The revolution of 1848 modified Austria's repressive policies somewhat but until the Empire was defeated by Prussia in 1866, Austria exploited the province politically and economically, After 1866, Galicia became almost an autonomous state within Austria. Governed by landowners the region remained economically backward but the agrarian movement fostered nationalism and Krakow was strengthened in its position as the artistic, literary and intellectual centre for the whole country. In 1907 universal suffrage was introduced throughout Austria, and a new, educated class favoured democratisation and

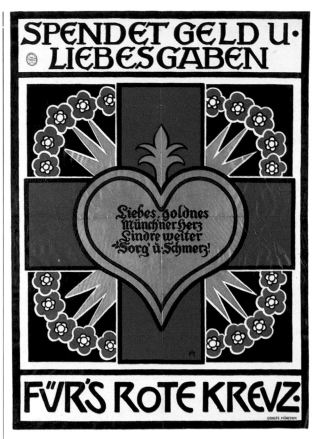

A. Münzer: *Spendet geld u. liebesgaben*, 191- , L of C

The poet and novelist Stanislaw Przybyszewski (1868-1927) returned to Krakow in 1898, after visiting Berlin, Scandinavia, Paris and Spain. Full of the latest news of artistic developments he encouraged Polish enthusiasm for Art Nouveau, which developed fully in the graphic arts in Warsaw, Krakow and Lwow.

In Krakow in 1897 an association of artists called the Sztuka (Art) was founded; the group, not all of whom lived in Krakow, kept in close contact with each other and with artists abroad including Przybyszewski's friend Munch. The group wished to exhibit the finest works of art and these were to be carefully selected. Krakow's School of Fine Arts (after 1900 called the Academy) drew artists from all three provinces. The cultural magazine *Czas* (Time) was published in Krakow, as was *Zycie* (Life). Przybyszewski became the editor of *Zycie* for two years from 1898, his art editor was Wyspianski.

Stanislaw Wyspianski (1869-1907) was extraordinarily versatile: painter, designer, typographer, poet and superb dramatist. Born in Krakow, he studied politics and philosophy at the university and painting with Matejko at the School of Fine Arts. While a student he travelled on a grant to France, Italy, Germany and Switzerland. From 1891 to 1894 he studied at the Académie Colarossi in Paris and made friends with Mucha and Gauguin, both of whose work thereafter was important for him, as well as for his older compatriot Wladyslaw Slewinski. Wyspianski was also influenced by the work of Degas, Eckmann, Bonnard and Toulouse-Lautrec. His interest in the Pre-Raphaelites is demonstrated by his stained-glass designs. Like most of his confrères in Paris, Wyspianski was particularly interested by Japanese prints.

Dziewczyna z kozikiem (Girl with pocket-knife) which Wyspianski painted in 1893 was the first truly Art Nouveau painting executed in Poland. Always at the forefront of artistic development, Wyspianski was remarkably prolific; he painted numerous portraits, including the brooding, intense self-portrait of 1894. After his return to Poland he painted frescoes in the Franciscan church in Krakow, designed stained-glass windows for the cathedral of Lwow and other churches, and designed sets and costumes for his own plays. The stained-glass designs

industrialisation.

Krakow was the ancient capital of the country and national feeling there was strong. The turn of the century was a time of great cultural activity in the theatre, literature and art. The movement Mloda Polska (Young Poland), also known as neo-Romanticism, like Symbolism in France was international in sympathy, but its adherents were united by their desire for national political and cultural unity.

Art Nouveau (in Polish Secesja) was for Poland an imported style rather than a style which developed locally as it had done in France and England. Nevertheless Poles were enthusiastic about it, with remarkable results. There is, even now, much Art Nouveau architecture extant, particularly in Krakow, Lwow, Poznan, Warsaw, Lublin, Vilnius and, most of all, Lodz. That city expanded and prospered with the successful textile industry and the inhabitants wanted to build in the latest fashion.

Anon.: Front page Czas
Krakow, 1896, NG
Warsaw

are particular1y alive and dramatic.

Wyspianski actively promulgated the idea of art in everyday life, encouraging the idea that mass-produced products can be well-designed. Always interested in folk-lore he used motifs from peasant art whenever possible. He designed several interiors and all their contents successfully combining Art Nouveau with a regional style, *podhalanski*. His interest in folk-art is also evident in his graphic designs. The floral motifs he used so often in the pages of *Zycie* were derived from his own magnificent flower drawings. His illustrations for *Iliada* show the curving lines and emphasis on women's hair typical of Art Nouveau.

Wyspianski was strongly influenced by his compatriot Wladyslaw Slewinski (1854-1918), who went to France in 1888. After several years in Paris, when he became a member of the circle around Gauguin, he spent most of his time in Brittany, living in his villa at Le Pouldu from 1895 to 1905. During the next five years he moved between Krakow, Poronin (near Zakopane, in the Tatra mountains) and Warsaw where he was professor at the School of Fine Arts for two years, returning then to France. Slewinski's attractive, decorative paintings are important because he helped disseminate the new ideas emerging from France through Eastern Europe.

Jan Bukowski (1873-1943) continued Wyspianski's work in book design. A successful, prolific artist, he had a considerable influence on Polish graphics. Bukowski studied law at the university in Krakow and then moved to the School of Fine Arts; he travelled to Germany, Italy and France, where he knew Gauguin, Mucha and Wyspianski. In 1900 he received a scholarship for study in Munich. The next year he joined the Sztuka in Krakow, and was one of the founder members of the Polska Sztuka Stosowana (Polish Applied Arts) with Jozef Czajkowski (1872- 1947), Karol Tichy (1871-1939), Karol Frycz (1877-1963) and Edward Trojanowski (1873-1930). Bukowski directed the Krakow University Press from 1904 to 1915, and from 1912 was a professor at the Krakow School of Arts and Crafts.

Bukowski's earlier works were mostly oils and watercolours. Later he received many ecclesiastical commissions for frescoes (these are influenced in style by Polish folk-art), mosaics and stained-glass windows. At the same time he was designing textiles, batik, book-bindings, tapestries and interiors. His graphic designs were probably the most influential and include numerous books which demonstrate his interest in William Morris's work, but they have an individual liveliness and vitality of their own. Bukowski participated in many exhibitions, wrote numerous articles, and had a profound effect on the development of graphic art in Poland.

Like Bukowski, Jozef Mehoffer (1869-1946)

studied law at the university in Krakow and then studied art at the School of Fine Arts under Matejko. At this time he was assisting Wyspianski with the frescoes in St.Mary's Church, Krakow. In 1889, after two years' study, he moved to Vienna and enrolled at the University and the Academy of Fine Arts. Having graduated in law, he went to Paris and studied at the Académie Colarossi and the Ecole des Beaux-Arts with Bonnat. In 1894 he won the international competition for the stained-glass windows in the Collegiate church in Freiburg. Execution took many years and his work changed stylistically, during the 1890s, becoming more Art Nouveau. After returning to Krakow for a time he spent another year in Paris finally settling in Krakow in 1897. In 1900 he became an assistant professor at the School of Fine Arts, and professor in 1902. Later he was several times appointed Rector. He received a number of ecclesiastical commissions, and designed books, posters, illustrations and vignettes for 'Chimera and Zycie, printed ephemera and for the theatre. Mehoffer's style changed during the course of his long career but was always balanced and richly-coloured; his pictures and graphic designs are attractive and charming.

Jacek Malczewski (1854-1929) studied at the Ecole des Beaux Arts in Paris from 1874 for three years, entered the School of Fine Arts in Krakow when he returned to Poland and the same year exhibited at the Salony Sztuk Pieknych (Chamber of Fine Arts) exhibition. In 1879 he left the School; his interests developed from folk-art to *sybirska* (conventionally realistic pictures, mostly with a Siberian winter theme) to Symbolism. The fantastic elements in his paintings were important to later Polish Art Nouveau artists. He taught at the Academy from 1896 to 1900, and again after 1911 for some time interrupted by a year or so in Vienna.

Another Symbolist graphic artist was Witold Wojtkiewicz (1879-1909) who studied at the Warsaw School of Drawing and at the Academy of Fine Arts in Krakow. He began as a satirist but gradually his work turned melancholy and strange. There are numerous drawings of the street-circus and extraordinary illustrations for books of fairy-tales with fantastic figures set in realistic landscapes. The influence of Toorop's *Three Brides* and of Beardsley's

work is particularly clear in Wojkiewicz's graphic work for various magazines, including *Nasz Kraj* (Our Country) published in Lwow.

Adolf Münzer (1870-1952) also illustrated books of fairy-tales but in a more conventional style. A painter and designer, his graphic work includes posters and illustrations for *Jugend*. Born in Pszczyna, in southern Poland, he attended the Academy in Munich and then studied in Paris from 1900 to 1902, returning to Munich to work until he was appointed Professor at the Academy in Düsseldorf. While in Munich he was a member of the Scholle group.

One of the co-founders of the Scholle group in 1899, Fritz Erler (1868-1940) was born near Wroclaw, where he studied art before attending the Académie Julian in Paris. After returning briefly to Wroclaw, he moved to Munich to pursue his successful career as a painter, illustrator (including the first cover of *Jugend*) and interior decorator. In 1898 Erler's early Jugendstil designs for the house of his patron Dr. Albert Neisser were much admired. Later in his career he painted numerous murals and

E. Oken: Cover for *Chimera*, 1902, NG Warsaw

portraits.

Born near Warsaw, Edward Okun (1872-1945) studied in Warsaw, Krakow, Munich and Paris. From 1898 to 1921 he lived in Italy and then returned to Warsaw where he later became a professor at the School of Fine Arts. He painted landscapes, portraits and some fantastic pictures, as well as many illustrations for books and magazines.

Ephraim Lilien (1874-1925) was another very prolific illustrator who designed for *Pan, Jugend* and numerous other magazines and newspapers. Born in Drogobych, in the area of Lwow, he studied briefly in Krakow, after working for a sign-painter, and then won a competition in Drogobych. In 1896 he moved to Munich, where he worked on a number of socialist publications, and then on to Berlin. In 1902 he founded the Jüdischer Verlag. Lilien was much involved in art education in Palestine and, in 1906, when a School of Applied Arts was opened in Jerusalem, he was responsible for much of the construction. Lilien designed a great many book illustrations throughout his career; earlier influenced by Aubrey Beardsley, he went on to find his own style, much admired by his contemporaries including Stefan Zweig.

One of the most prolific Art Nouveau artists in Poland, Stanislaw Debicki (1866-1924) studied in Lwow, Krakow, Munich and Paris, returning to Krakow to become teacher and then, in 1911, professor at the Krakow Academy of Fine Arts. Debicki belonged to the Vienna Secession and was a leader of the Sztuka. One of the most outstanding graphic artists of the time, he designed numerous book and magazine illustrations and worked in the theatre.

Another artist working in the Art Nouveau style was Wojciech Weiss, who designed posters and illustrations for books and magazines, especially for *Mlodosc* (Youth) and *Zycie* (Life). Various other younger artists were also influenced by Wyspianski's art; Jan Rembowski (1879-1923), Tymon Niesiolowski (1882-1965), Leopold Gottlieb and Apoloniusz Kedzierski (1861-1939).

Ferdynand Ruszczyc (1870-1936) was a professor at the Warsaw Academy of Fine Art from 1904 to 1906 and then worked in Krakow and, later, in Vilnius. Ruszczyc was very able technically and a distinguished teacher. Interestingly, he influenced the Lithuanian artist Mikalojus Konstantinas Cziurlonis (1875-1911). There is a strong Art Nouveau element in his work. One of Poland's leading Symbolists he designed covers and graphics for Chimera, an important Symbolist magazine, which was started in 1901 by Zenon Przesmycki (whose nom de plume was "Miriam"). The vignettes, illustrations and typographical designs were by Mehoffer, Okun, Antoni Procajlowicz (1876-1949), Stanislaw Turbia-Krysztalowicz and Franciszek Wojtala. The designs were almost all by Poles but there were some articles about foreign artists including Rossetti, Burne-Jones, Moreau, Redon, Beardsley, Vallotton, and about Japanese prints. The magazine promulgated the idea of "art for art's sake" but was unpopular at the time of the 1905 revolution because it was felt to be elitist and anti-democratic. In 1907 it faded away.

Kazimierz Stabrowski (1869-1929), Antoni Gawinski (1876-1954), Antoni Procajlowicz and Bonawentura Lenart (1881- ?) were all involved in book and magazine design and illustration. In 1913 Lenart was one of the artists who set up the Warsztaty Krakowskie (Krakow Workshop), which was similar to the Wiener Werkstätte. Others in the group were Wojciech Jastrzebowski (1884-1963), Antoni Buszek, Karol and Zofia Stryjenski. Assisted by the Miejskie Muzeum Techniczno-Przemyslowe (City Technical-Industrial Museum), the group both designed and executed carpets, batiks, toys, metalwork and furniture. Subsequently influenced by Expressionism, their style changed from curvilinear to severely geometric.

Secesja in Poland was enthusiastically received by artists and patrons so that many remarkable works of art were produced and appreciated by contemporaries and up to the present day.

Russia

Following the emancipation of serfs in 1861, the greatest reform of many during Alexander II's reign, the country advanced rapidly towards industrialisation. Local government and administration became much more efficient and the law and the armed forces were reformed. The universities were opened to all students, including women, and there were numerous exchanges with universities abroad.

After the Russo-Turkish War, Russia regained lost territory and acquired Turkistan (1867) and Transcaspia (1884). In the Far East the territory acquired by the Treaty of Ai-Hun included the site of Vladivostok. In 1867 Alaska was sold to the United States for $7,200,000.

During the twenty years before 1876 the railway line-distance multiplied almost twenty times, factory-production nearly trebled, coal production increased twenty times, and the number of workmen grew from 419,000 to 769,000. After emancipation many peasants migrated. The population more than doubled between 1870 and 1912, and was 170 million, compared to the German Empire's 65 million and the United Kingdom's 45 million.

Moscow was the largest manufacturing town in Russia with a population of 1,617,000 in 1912 and had nine main railway stations. Railroads were all, except for the Trans-Siberian line, built by private enterprise like railroads in Great Britain. One of the railroad barons Savva Mamontov became a great patron of the arts. A number of merchant princes were major art-collectors, including Sergei Schukin, Savva Morozov and Tretyakov.

When Alexander III succeeded his assassinated father in 1881, some new reforms were carried out but there was increased Russification, the press was gagged, and the populist revolutionary movement was suppressed. Although Russia was still largely an agrarian country it was gradually being industrialised; steel production, for example, had reached half that of Great Britain by 1910.

The last Tsar, Nicholas II, succeeded his father in 1894 and soon disappointed those who had hoped for reforms. He continued with the policy of Russification and ruled autocratically but indecisively. At the turn of the century there was an industrial depression, with a rise in unemployment, and a number of strikes. Political opposition revived. The non-Russian nationalities resented various governmental actions and nationalist movements developed in Estonia, Latvia, Lithuania, Poland and the Ukraine. The Armenians and the Finns were also restive.

The Russo-Japanese war ended disastrously with the loss of the Baltic fleet dispatched to the Far East in 1905. Three months earlier troops had fired on a large crowd of peacefully demonstrating workers in front of the Winter Palace in St.Petersburg. Two hundred were killed and about two thousand wounded. This was widely condemned and during the spring and summer there were agrarian riots, marches and a general strike. Finally the Tsar agreed to an elected legislative assembly, the Duma, and made a number of reforms. After various problems

the emperor dissolved the Duma and a second Duma was elected and promptly dissolved in its turn. The situation had improved somewhat in that censorship had almost ceased, political parties and trade unions were legalised and there were agricultural reforms. The economy recovered a little and the industrial sector grew considerably. Stolypin, the prime minister, continued the policy of Russification, however.In 1914 Russia entered the World War. Terrible casualties, retreats in 1915 and 1916, the government's incompetence, and economic difficulties fuelled the revolution of 1917, which ended the Romanov dynasty.

The last decades of the nineteenth century were a time of experimentation, of philosophical discussion, of debate between the Westernisers and the Slavophiles, of numerous new periodicals and newspapers, of cultural and scientific innovations. The intelligentsia were a powerful social and political force by this time.

Like the writers and musicians of the day, many artists wanted to paint realistic subjects and to return to their roots in the land. The Academy of Fine Arts in St.Petersburg had become a rigid, inflexible organisation and, in 1863, a group of artists resigned from the Academy to form the St.Petersburg Artel (community) of Artists. Several of the fourteen, with eleven artists from Moscow, in 1870 formed the Association of circulating Exhibitions, who soon became known as the Peredvizhniki (the Wanderers). Opposed to the narrow dogmatism of the Academy they aimed for realism, a national culture and social consciousness. The travelling exhibitions started in St.Petersburg and Moscow and then went on to the provinces. The Peredvizhniki were helped and encouraged from the start by Pavel Tretyakov, a Moscow merchant and millowner who founded a national museum of Russian art in Moscow, still called the Tretyakov Gallery today. When he succeeded to the throne in 1881, Alexander III continued the policy of Russification, adopting the Peredvizhniki as the national school of art and in 1889 the Peredvizhniki were asked to assist with the reorganisation of the Academy of Fine Arts. To the next generation of artists the work of the Peredvizhniki seemed conventional and artistically irrelevant although some admired their success.

Two artists whose work came between the Peredvizhniki and their artistic successors were Mikhail Vasilievich Nesterov (1862-1942) and Mikhail Aleksandrovitch Vrubel (1856-1911). Nesterov attended both the Moscow School of Painting, Sculpture and Architecture and the St.Petersburg Academy achieving membership of the Academy in 1898. Chiefly known as a religious painter, he also painted portraits, genre scenes and landscapes. He executed murals in St.Vladimir's Cathedral, Kiev, the Cathedral of the Resurrection in St.Petersburg and in the Marfo-Marinsky Monastery in Moscow. Nesterov's religious paintings are idealistic and symbolic, very much influenced by Puvis de Chavannes. He spent some time on Savva Mamontov's country estate.

Mamontov was one of a number of businessmen who wanted to encourage native art because they realised that the folk traditions were gradually disappearing. He bought Abramtsevo, an estate outside Moscow, which had once belonged to Sergei Aksakov the writer, in 1870. Abramtsevo became a great gathering-place for the leading artists and musicians of the time. The Mamontovs built a hospital and a school and collected native art and artefacts. The church they built, in fourteenth-century Novgorod style, on the estate was researched, designed and decorated by the Mamontovs and their friends. The building was important in the revival of medieval art and architecture, as was the church on the estate of Princess Tenisheva at Talashkino near Smolensk. In the studios at Talashkino there was instruction in manuscript illumination and choral singing as well as traditional crafts. As part of the movement to encourage arts and crafts, a number of artists were commissioned by the *zemstvo* (local council) to make designs. One such artist was Maria Yakunchikova (1870-1902) whose graphic designs are very much in the Russian Art Nouveau style.

Mikhail Aleksandrovich Vrubel (1856-1911) was one of Russia's greatest artists. Born at Omsk of Polish and Danish descent, he travelled in France and Italy, spending some time in Venice, before and after studying at the Academy in St. Petersburg under Pavel Chistiakov, having begun his studies by

reading philosophy at the University of St.Petersburg. Like Aubrey Beardsley, Vrubel was particularly interested by Greek vase-painting. An intellectual, classical scholar, his art historical studies made him particularly suited to restoring the murals of St.Cyril at Kiev. Vrubel found in Byzantine art a two-dimensional use of line which particularly appealed to him, and in Venetian art he found colour. In 1885 he went to Odessa but had difficulty finding work. In 1887 Victor Vasnetsov won the competition for the murals at the new Cathedral of St. Vladimir at Kiev, which was bitterly disappointing for Vrubel. His friend, Valentin Serov (1865-1911) introduced him to Savva Mamontov whom he knew well, having grown up at Abramtsevo. Serov was a gifted landscape painter and was well-known later for his brilliant, striking portraits. As a result of this introduction to Mamontov, Vrubel became interested in applied art, especially stage design, he also painted a number of portraits of his wife, the celebrated singer Nadezhda Zabela, which are richly-surfaced, sad and haunting.

Vrubel was particularly interested in Art Nouveau and in the work of the French Symbolists, especially Gustave Moreau, echoes of whose work can be seen in the illustrations for Lermontov's poem *The Demon*, one of his few commissions. He was deeply interested by Slavonic mythology and the image of the demon haunted him. In the remarkably imaginative watercolours Vrubel painted during his last working years he was gradually moving towards Cubism; the abstract, dynamic shapes unlike work by his Russian contemporaries made him the great precursor of Russia's finest modern painters.

Alexander Benois (1870-1960) was the leader of a schoolboy society for "self- education" in the late 1880s. Other members included Dmitri Filosofov, interested more in literature, Konstantin Somov, son of the Director of the Hermitage Museum and Walter Nuvel who was the most musical of the group. In 1890 these friends left school. During this year they were joined by a young cousin of Filosofov's from the country called Sergei Diaghilev (1872-1929). Benois met an artist called Lev Rosenberg (better known as Léon Bakst), while attending evening classes at the St. Petersburg Academy, who became a popular member of the group. Before attending university most of the group went abroad for a year; Benois to Munich, Diaghilev and Filosofov to Paris.

On their return from abroad, they were joined by Valentin Serov and Konstantin Korovin (1861-1939), who also knew the Mamontovs well and who were soon followed by Nicholas Roerich (1874-1917), a keen archaeologist. In 1893 Charles Birlé, a young French diplomat, joined the group for a time and introduced them to the work of Gauguin, Seurat and Van Gogh as well as the Impressionists. Birlé's half-English friend, Alfred Nurok, introduced them to the art of T. T. Heine, Steinlen and Aubrey Beardsley, whose work became extremely influential.

In 1896 Somov, Benois and his nephew Evgenii Lanceray (1875-1946) went to Paris. Most of the group travelled, for example, Mstislav Dobuzhinsky (1875-1957) spent two years in Munich. Diaghilev had visited France the year before and had collected a number of paintings. In 1897 he organised his first exhibitions: *Scandinavian Painters* and *English and German Watercolours*. Fired with enthusiasm, Diaghilev persuaded Benois to return to Russia to help him launch a new magazine, to be called *Mir Iskusstva* (World of Art), and a series of annual exhibitions.

On March 23 1898 Diaghilev and the financial backers Savva Mamontov and Princess Maria Tenisheva submitted a printed prospectus to the government department which regulated printed publications. The proposed journal was to contain: 1. A section on fine arts, with art criticism. 2. A section on applied art and art industry. 3. A section with an "Artistic Chronicle". It was envisaged as a popular magazine similar to *The Studio*, to be low-priced, non-specialised and providing designs for craftsmen. The group wanted to unite "pure art" and applied art, to renew appreciation of the art of the past, especially Russian art, and to improve current standards by making contemporary European art more widely known.

Comparable with the Nabis in many ways, the group were devoted to art for art's sake and to the pursuit of individualism. Benois designed the eagle emblem for the magazine and described it as "above all earthly things, above the stars, there it reigns proud, secret and lonely as on a snowy mountain

peak". The magazine reflected their different interests. Filosofov was in charge of production and made a splendid job of it, including the eighteenth-century matrices, and the special paper. The editors were Benois, Diaghilev and Somov. Reading the magazine one finds a mixture of articles on the Slavic revival with many illustrations of work done at Abramtsevo and Talashkino and accounts of the work of Art Nouveau artists and the Symbolists. In the later issues there are articles about the Post-Impressionists, Gauguin, Van Gogh and Cézanne.In an article Benois wrote in 1910 he attributed the revival of the graphic arts (particularly book illustration) to *Mir skusstva*.

To a considerable extent this was correct but the International Exhibition of Posters held in St. Petersburg in 1897 was very influential for Russian graphic design. The posters exhibited included works by Grasset, Toulouse-Lautrec, Forain and Heine. Numerous posters were designed subsequently; most of those in the Art Nouveau style were for exhibitions, theatres and magazines like the placard of 1899 for *Niva*, a literary journal, by Elena Samokich-Soudkovskaya (1860-1924) and posters by Nikolai Andreev (1873-1932). The posters by Bakst and Somov are subtle and attractive; Bakst's later posters such as *Caryathisare* more dramatic.

After the 1900 exhibition the *Mir Iskusstva* shows became somewhat less international, with greater emphasis on Russian art. In 1912 there was a memorial exhibition, within the main show, for Mikolojus Ciurlionis the composer-painter who worked in St. Petersburg from 1906 to his death, whose musical abstract paintings are remarkable for their time. Serov and Korovin joined the original members after a couple of years, and then a number of younger artists joined the group including D. S. Stelletsky (1875-1944) and Ivan Bilibine (1876-1942) whose graphic art, influenced by Japanese prints but firmly based in the Russian tradition, is both powerful and lyrical. The younger members of the Moscow school included Igor Grabar (1871-1960), Pavel Kuznetsov (1878-1968) and Nikolai Sapunov (1880-1912). The Russian symbolist Victor Borisov-Musatov (1870-1905) in his nostalgic, poetic works, which were important for Kandinsky's early paintings, also inspired the "Blue Rose"

Symbolist painters, who were influenced by Vrubel's art and ideas.

In 1905 Diaghilev organised a very large exhibition of Russian portraits. This national success was followed by the *Exposition d'art russe* at the Salon d'Automne in Paris in 1906. This exhibition was also very successful. The exhibition showed examples of all periods of Russian art, mostly eighteenth and nineteenth-century but including works by some of the youngest Moscow artists like Mikhail Larionov (1881-1964) and Natalia Goncharova (1881-1962). Benois, Diaghilev and Bakst concentrated on the theatre and ballet in Paris from this time on, and their achievements in those fields are beyond the scope of this book.

After the magazine *Mir Iskusst* ended, various other art magazines were founded in a remarkable flowering of periodicals, including *Apollon*, in which all the arts were integrated. One of the most important of these was *Zolotoïe Rouno* (The Golden Fleece), which organised three important exhibitions. As the journal of the 'Blue Rose' group the magazine fulfilled the same role as *Mir Iskusstva*, and some of the contributors were the same. The Armenian painter Martiros Saryan (1880-1972) was one of the most original of the 'Blue Rose' group. The *Mir Iskusstva* group was replaced to some extent by the 'Union of Russian Artists', an exhibiting society which was formed in 1903, and then replaced in its turn by the 'Blue Rose' group in 1906.

In 1910 the groups which were exhibiting in various cities joined together as the 'Union of Youth', which met twice a year. Vladimir Izdebsky arranged a Salon in Odessa which introduced the Munich Secession into Russia. Vassily Kandinsky (1886-1944), Alexei Yavlensky (1864-1941) and Gabriele Münter (1877-1962) had founded the Neue Künstlervereinigung in Munich in 1909,and they joined with several other artists to form the 'Blaue Reiter' group. Much of Kandinsky's work was inspired by Russian folk art (including *lubki*) and by Art Nouveau.

Scandinavia

At the turn of the century the Nordic countries became modern, industrial nations. Norway achieved independence from Sweden in 1905 when Prince Charles of Denmark, married to King Edward VII of Great Britain's daughter Maude, became King Haakon VII. The social and political reforms which had been put in hand before independence continued, for example universal political suffrage began in 1913. To make use of Norway's vast water resources, Norsk Hydro was founded in 1905 and the country was swiftly industrialised, with far-reaching economic and social results. Starting in 1854, an excellent railway system had been established and communications, necessary to such a spread-out country, were excellent.

In spite of widespread emigration, mostly to America, the cities grew considerably; Kristiania (Oslo) having a population of about 230,000 in 1900. Interestingly, in Scandinavia even the largest industrial cities were set in wild, rugged country.

By 1900 nearly a third of the population of Sweden were engaged in commerce and industry. Stockholm had a population of about 400,000. From the 1850s there had been much emigration, almost all to America, partly because the protectionist trade policy (adopted in self-defence against cheap grain from Russia and America) had resulted in an agrarian depression, and partly because the birthrate was high. The geography and climate of the country made all forms of communication extremely important. Natural waterways were extended by canals and the state from the outset was actively

involved in the construction of railways.

Dissolution of the union with Norway led to political changes in Sweden and increasing industrialisation promoted a number of social and

O. Holmboe: *Norwegen*, 1900, L of C

political reforms. Gustavus V, who succeeded to the throne in 1907, proved to be a capable, farsighted monarch who assisted the passage of reforms through the Riksdag, and helped establish a national defence plan as well.

In Denmark a number of reforms were carried through the Rigsdag at the turn of the century. From the 1870s Denmark became an industrialised nation, having been an agrarian country, with some cottage industry, until then. Denmark was not as badly hurt as other countries by cheap American and Russian grain because her farmers were able to increase production and crop yield and to establish co-operatives for production and export of bacon and dairy products. Transport, by road, rail and sea, was excellent for the time, as were Communications. Denmark was a world leader in the change to motor-driven ships, which contributed significantly to the country's prosperity.

From 1809 to 1917 Finland was a Russian grand duchy. Finnish autonomy increased during the middle years of the nineteenth century until Alexander II imposed a harsh system of Russification, which was very much resented, so that eventually the Eduskunta in Helsinki adopted the Declaration of Independence. After the civil war which ensued, many social reforms were carried out and after 1917 the republic gradually reorganised the administration and the economy, which even now is based to a considerable extent on the use of land. Finnish nationalism always has been inextricably bound up with her rich and artistically immensely influential folk culture and literature, which includes the *Kalevala* (1849), a great national epic poem, compiled by Elias Lönnrot.

When considering Scandinavian art contemporary literature needs to be borne in mind. Early Scandinavian literature is, in essence, Icelandic poetry which has, rightly, been famous for a thousand years. From the end of the fourteenth century Iceland was ruled by and from Denmark, becoming an independent republic again in 1944. During the nineteenth century the Independence movement, headed by Jon Sigurdsson (1811-79), aimed for complete social, Economic and constitutional reform. In spite of massive emigration, mostly to Canada, there were considerable economic

and educational improvements and after the new constitution of 1903, there was even more progress made particularly affecting communications, the fishing industry, foreign trade and agriculture.

The five Scandinavian countries, while largely independent and with different languages (Swedish and English are the two *lingua franca*), were united by common cultural, historical, geographical and climatic characteristics, by the Lutheran Church and by the nationalism endemic in Europe at the time. One could say that their art is united by the quality of light, and distinctive restraint and by a particular concern with nature in all its forms. In Nordic *stämning* (a combination of mood and atmosphere) painting light and nature are used to express abstract concepts such as death, loneliness, solitude, spiritual heritage. *Stämning* painting is sometimes animistic; this anthropomorphic pantheism is exemplified in literary terms by Knut Hamsun's *Pan* (1894).

Hamsun was well acquainted with the painter Edvard Munch (1863-1944), one of the great artists of his generation, in whom the transition between Post-Impressionism and Expressionism is apparent. A number of Munch's early works exhibit the linear serpentina of Art Nouveau; his prints have an unequalled grandeur, psychological insight and emotional power, thus transcending the decorative, organic designs of most Art Nouveau works.

The dramatic intensity of Munch's work is rooted in his sad, bereaved childhood in Kristiania; all his life he was haunted by illness and death. After giving up the engineering training his father had arranged for him, Munch entered the Royal School of Drawing in 1881. In 1882 a number of artists who opposed the official Art Association held their own exhibition, known as the Autumn exhibition. Munch exhibited the next year with them after he began sharing a studio with six colleagues, under the artistic supervision of Christian Krohg the realist painter.

Through him he came to know the Bohemian group of Kristiania, including the writer Hans Jaeger and Karl Jensen-Hjell, the painter. In 1885 Frits Thaulow (Gauguin's brother-in-law), whose "Open Air Academy" Munch had attended at Modum, sent him to Antwerp and Paris for three weeks' study.

In 1889 Munch had his first one-man exhibition,

at the Students' Association in Oslo and, having been awarded his first State scholarship, went to Paris to study with Léon Bonnat. He spent the next few years in Paris and Nice (returning to Norway each summer) coming into contact with the avant-garde artists of the time. The new ideas and techniques he encountered in France had a profound effect on his art.

After a one-man exhibition in the Norwegian capital in 1892, Munch was invited to exhibit at the Verein Berliner Künstler, whose Director was the Norwegian painter Adelsten Normann. The exhibition caused a furore and was closed after a few days, one of a series of events which so angered a group of artists, led by Max Liebermann, that they formed a new association. Later they, with others, formed the Berlin Secession. Munch became the "man of the moment" and was subsequently asked to exhibit in Cologne and Düsseldorf. He settled in Berlin, where his friends, who met regularly at the tavern Zum Schwarzen Ferkel, included Stanislaw Przybyszewski and Dagny Juell (later his wife), Julius Meier- Graefe, August Strindberg (1849-1912), whom we know as an author and playwright but who thought of himself as primarily an artist, Gustav Vigeland the sculptor and Axel Gallén (1865-1931).

From the early 1880s to his nervous breakdown in 1909, Munch painted most of the pictures belonging to the great *Frieze of Life*, a series which presented a picture of man's whole existence, a poem of life, love and death. Much of the series was shown at the Berlin Secession in 1902. The lines of the compositions are reminiscent of Art Nouveau but have a forcefulness and tension characteristic of Munch.

While he was in Berlin in 1894 Munch made his first etchings, possibly fired by his enthusiasm for Max Klinger's work, and perhaps from interest in the work of the young Käthe Kollwitz. In Paris in 1896 Munch printed his first colour lithographs and woodcuts, a medium particularly suited to his art; he developed the expressive possibilities further than any of his contemporaries and inspired the next generation. After mastering all the graphic media he used whichever one suited him at that moment often exploring the possibilities of some subjects several times, like *The Sick Child*. In his lithographs Munch employs a rhythmical, expressive line, particularly evident in *Release* (1896), *Attraction* (1896), *Madonna* (1895 and 1902), *Lovers in the Waves* (1896). This is also seen in some of the other prints, notably the woodcuts *In Man's Brain* (1897) and *The Maiden and the Heart* (1899).

During the 1890s Munch had work published in *Pan* and *La Revue Blanche*, a lithograph was included in Vollard's *Album des peintres graveurs* and he had a number of exhibitions, as well as exhibiting at Les Indépendants and at Siegfried Bing's Salon de l'Art Nouveau. His work was appreciated in Paris but after 1902, when he exhibited at the Berlin Secession, he had greater success in Germany. The list of his exhibitions is remarkably long and includes some in Scandinavia, the United States, France, Belgium, Austria, Italy, Russia and Czechoslovakia. The exhibition of 1905 in Prague was a great success. The next year he visited Henry van de Velde in Weimar. Throughout his career his art changed and evolved; after his breakdown in 1908, becoming more colourful, formal and monumental and was, at last, greatly respected and admired.

Among Norwegian artists working in the Art Nouveau style were Othar Holmboe, Frida Hansen (1855-1931), G. Laerum and Gerhard Munthe (1849-1929), who studied in Munich and Düsseldorf and who fused the international style with his own attractive, decorative manner derived from folk-culture. The revival of Viking art (also known as dragon style or Old Nordic style) derived from medieval architecture and from archaeological finds is considered particularly Norwegian. Thorolf Holmboe (1866- 1935) studied in Kristiania then in Düsseldorf with Hans Gude (1825-1923) and later at Cormon's atelier in Paris during 1889 and 1890, travelling meanwhile in Italy, Sweden and the United States. A successful painter, illustrator and designer, whose graphic designs are deeply influenced by his study of Japanese prints, he showed at many international exhibitions.

In 1895 Munch exhibited with Axel Gallén (from 1904 known as Akseli Gallen-Kallela) who was the leading Finnish exponent of Art Nouveau. In 1882 the Finska Konstföreningen (Finnish Art Society) provoked a rebellion when it selected paintings for the Russian state exhibition without consulting any

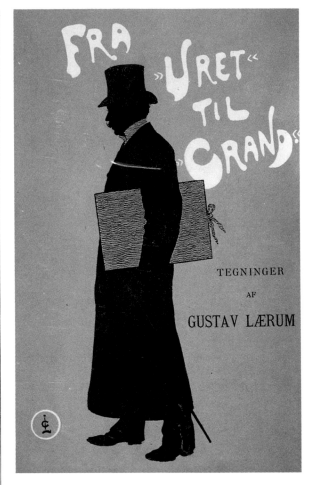

G. Lærum: *Fra Uret til Grand*, 190-, L of C

of the artists involved, a number of whom set up an alternative exhibition which lasted until Albert Edelfelt (1854-1905) became director of the Finska Konstföreningen in 1903. Edelfelt's interesting and attractive work was influenced by Manet, Bastien-Lepage and *plein air* painting, like so many Nordic artists to whom light was vitally important.

Light is a vital element of the work of Gallen-Kallela, evident in, for example, *Waterfall at Mäntykoski* (1892-3), a wonderful, almost mystical landscape with an integral frame, symbolising the music of nature. Gallen-Kallela's earlier *plein-air* style is still in evidence here. He started his artistic studies at the Drawing School of the Finnish Fine Arts Association, moving to Adolf von Becker's private art school, where apparently he paid for his studies by illustrating temperance tracts, which must have

been useful experience. Late in 1884 he went to Paris attending the Académie Julian and, subsequently, Cormon's telier.

Gallen-Kallela began painting scenes from the *Kalevala* while he was in Paris and in 1890 he travelled with his friend Louis Sparre (1863-1964) to Karelia, on the eastern border, to learn more about ancient Finnish culture. This journey started the Karelian movement among his confrères, reinforcing both nationalism and the "return to nature" ideas current among artists in the 1890s.

Georg Brandes (1842-1927), an aesthetician, writer and critic who was immensely influential in the cultural life of late nineteenth-century Scandinavia, advocated realism in art. Among those who enthusiastically accepted his ideas were the Skagen painters, including Henrik Ibsen (1828-1906) and August Strindberg (1849-1912). Skagen in Denmark was one of the main Nordic artistic colonies of the time along with Varberg in Sweden, Fleskum in Norway, and Onningeby on Lemland in the Åland Islands. In the 1890s Gallen-Kallela spent much time in the remoter parts of his country, especially after a disappointing visit to Paris in 1892 when reviews of his *Aino Triptych* were not favourable. He then changed his style, absorbing many of the tenets of Synthetism and Symbolism to create decorative, stylised, unified and monumental paintings, which were extremely influential.

Gallen-Kallela's graphic work was of equal importance in Finnish art; he was the first artist to make woodcuts and his interest in ancient Finnish art influenced the use of ribbon ornament by his contemporaries. During his travels in 1895, he was particularly interested by the new developments in graphic art in Berlin and contributed to *Pan*; in London he was more interested by the work of the Arts and Crafts Movement and his connections with England had an effect on the development of Scandinavian art. William Morris was sufficiently interested in the Icelandic sagas to travel there so the influences were two-way. Willy Finch (1854-1930) was born in Belgium of English parents and was one of the founders of Les XX. He moved to Finland in the 1890s and from 1902 was director of the ceramics division of Louis Sparre's Iris factory, and later taught in Helsinki thereby serving as

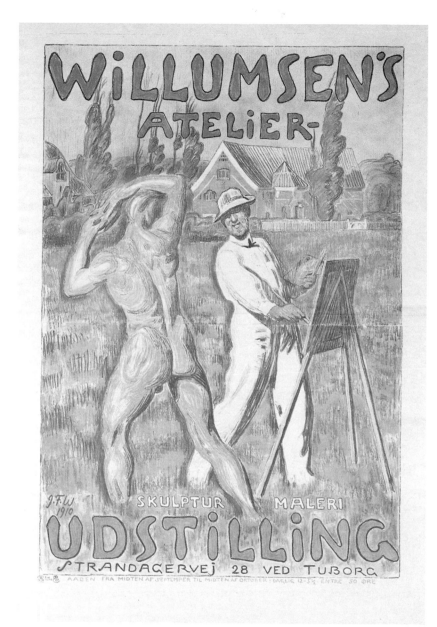

J. F. Willumsen:
Willumsen's Atelier,
1910, L of C

and continued travel his style changed, especially his use of colour. Later he was one of the Group of Seven and then an associate of die Brücke.

Gallen-Kallela's pupil, Hugo Simberg (1873-1917) studied first at the Drawing School of the Viipuri Art Association and then at the school of the Finnish Arts Association, teaching at both later. In the mid-1890s he studied with Gallen-Kallela who was one of the two major influences on his art, the other being Symbolism.

Gustaf Fjaestad (1868-1948), a Swedish Symbolist, was influenced by the work of the Varberg group. He studied with Bruno Liljefors (1860-1939) and Carl Larsson (1853-1919) after attending the Konstakademien in Stockholm. In 1897 he moved to Värmland and collected a group of artists around him, the Racken School. A successful painter of landscapes, he made numerous woodcuts at the turn of the century and designed tapestries and carpets.

Textiles are of primary interest in Jugend, the Swedish Art Nouveau style. The ideas of William Morris and the English Arts and Crafts Movement were widely disseminated by Ellen Key 1849-1926) in several books including *Skönhet für alla* (Beauty for Everyone), 1899. the leading international periodicals, especially *The Studio,* were widely read in Sweden and were very influential, combined with the revival of the ancient folk art. One result of the movement towards reform was the establishment of the Konstnärsförbundet's School in 1886 by many leading Swedish artists. This survived until the end of the First World War. These artists included Anders Zorn (1860-1920) and Carl Larsson, the extremely gifted draughtsman from Stockholm, who studied at the Academy before travelling to France where he spent much of his time from 1877 to 1885. When he returned to Sweden he moved to the country house which is enchantingly shown in his attractive watercolours, published in 1899 in his book *Ett Hem* (A Home) which was, and is still very popular. Larsson also painted monumental paintings and frescoes; one of his most famous works is the Japanese-influenced self-portrait, in a red coat, with Art Nouveau swirls in the background. Larsson's pupil Wilhelm Köge (1889-1960) is best known as a poster designer, as were Richard Bergh (1858-1919),

another link between the English and Finnish Art Nouveau and Arts and Crafts movements.

Gallen-Kallela also designed furniture, textiles, metalwork, stained-glass and large-scale frescoes, as did his pupil Simberg. The Finnish pavilion at the 1900 Paris Exhibition (designed by Gesellius, Lindgren and Saarinen with frescoes by Gallen-Kallela) was much admired and Gallen-Kallela was awarded the Légion d'Honneur in 1902. With time

Arthur Sjögren (1874-1951) and Nils Kreuger (1858-1930).

Jens Ferdinand Willumsen (1863-1958) was a leading Scandinavian Art at the Kunstakadamiet in Copenhagen, he attended Kroyer's school and went on to Paris in 1888. During his second stay in Paris from 1890 to 1894, he became friendly with Maurice Denis and his circle, and with Gauguin who exerted a particularly important influence on him. In Copenhagen he joined the Frie Udstilling group which had been formed in 1891 by Thorvald Bindesboll the architect (1846-1908), Joachim Skovgaard (1856-1933), his brother Niels Skovgaard (1858-1938) and others. Willumsen's friend Emil Hansen (Nolde 1867-1956) spent some time in Copenhagen before leaving for Germany in 1906 when he joined Die Brücke.

One of Willumsen's best-known paintings, *Jotunheimen*, is Symbolist in feeling because the frame is an integral part of the painting so that the formal boundaries of the work no longer exist. The three-dimensional frame heightens the illusion. Willumsen's later work is remarkably Expressionist in style but was, surprisingly, uninfluential.

Scandinavian artists of the fin de siècle were strongly affected by international influences but they endeavoured to retain their cultural identity so that there is a clearly Nordic atmosphere and an unequalled feeling for light and nature in their work.

Spain

The International Exposition held in Barcelona in 1888 was the first held in Spain. Organised along the same lines as major exhibitions in London, Paris and other cities, it was intended to demonstrate Barcelona's forward-thinking modernity, independence and prosperity. The director of the Exposition was the second Marquis of Comillas, owner of the Compañia Transatàntica and brother-in- law of Eusebio Güell y Bacigalupi, a textile manufacturer, publisher, and important patron.

The chief city of Catalonia, Barcelona is a cultural and industrial centre, partly because it is a port and partly because it is situated on one of the two main Spanish rail lines. During the nineteenth century the manufacture of machinery was added to the older textile, iron and shipbuilding industries. The art industries of silversmithing, ironwork, furniture and glass making were expanded at this time, upholding the Catalonian tradition of workshop manufacture. The reduction in wine sales caused by the advent of phylloxera into Spanish vineyards slowed the rapid economic expansion of previous years. Between 1850 and 1900 the population of the city quadrupled to almost 600,000, France, England, Germany and the United States were the principal export markets at this time.

In 1886 Alfonso XII was succeeded by his son Alfonso XIII, born posthumously, who reigned until 1931 when the Second Republic was established. The first five years of the queen mother's regency saw the restoration of universal suffrage, Liberal rule, the civil code of 1889 and liberalisation of several

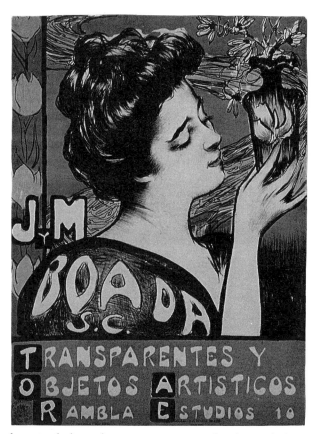

laws including those pertaining to freedom of the press.

In 1890 Canovas and the Conservative party returned to power, soon adopting a protectionist trade policy which only benefited heavy industry. The government had severe financial problems and

Ramón Casas i Carbó:
Rambla Estudios, 1900

113

Alexandre de Requier:
Juan Torra, 1899

Alexandre de Requier:
Napoleon, 1900

was not coping with numerous agricultural difficulties derived from an outdated land ownership system. Labour unrest grew especially in Catalonia, exacerbated by a wave of repression, which included the Montjuïc trial of anarchists, following the explosion of a bomb in Barcelona in June 1896 by persons never known. Canovas de Castillo was assassinated a year later in reprisal for the Montjuïc sentences.

The situation in Cuba, a Spanish colony, grew more and more threatening, a slump in sugar prices

having precipitated revolt followed by guerilla warfare in which the U.S. supported the rebels. In 1898 a crisis was precipitated by the explosion of the U.S. battleship 'Maine' in Havana harbour and war ensued. After the destruction of her Eastern and Caribbean fleets, Spain sued for peace. By the Treaty of Paris Spain gave up all rights to Cuba and Puerto Rico and ceded the Philippines and other islands to the U.S. in return for 20 million dollars. Several other islands were later sold to Germany and the Spanish Empire, apart from the African colonies, was finally at an end.

This disaster had a number of results; there was a renewed movement towards decentralisation so that the new Conservative government in Madrid appointed several Catalanist ministers. However these ministers, with Dr. Robert, newly-appointed Catalanist mayor of Barcelona, shortly resigned in protest at a profit tax imposed by the government to recoup lost colonial revenues. These problems solidified Catalanist opposition leading to the foundation of the Unió Regionalista, a breakaway group from the Conservative party, and the Centre Nacional Català, formed by some members of the Unió Catalanista.

The 'generation of 98' emerged with a new spirit of analysis and heartsearching to renovate the nation's literary and intellectual life. There were numerous long-overdue financial reforms made which improved the state of the economy and within Spain greater interest was taken in the African colonies. Another effect of the débâcle was that the Latin American countries became more sympathetic towards Spain. The Army, having a reduced empire to defend, began to meddle in politics again. There were religious controversies but the most immediate problem for the government was the economic situation in Catalonia arising from the loss of its traditional colonial markets. Unrest and several strikes culminated in the general strike of 1902, not long before Alfonso XIII was enthroned, on his sixteenth birthday. A period of governmental instability followed culminating in the "tragic week" of 1909 in Barcelona when much was destroyed in the city.

From this background came the movement known as Modernisme, the Spanish version of Art Nouveau. The movement's roots were in local tradition and

Alexandre de Requier:
3ra Exposicion de Bellas Artes, 1896

indigenous art; in their resistance to industrial, standardised art they were influenced by William Morris and the English Arts and Crafts Movement. The writings of John Ruskin were well known in Barcelona and fostered interest in Catalan Gothic. Other influences included Orientalism and contemporary developments elsewhere in Europe especially in Paris, London and Brussels. The renaissance in Catalan cultural life is clearly visible in the pages of a number of magazines including *La Renaixença*, published from 1871 to 1905, which embodied moderate Catalan opinion.

Generally speaking architects were the stars of Modernismo, the most famous being Lluis Domènech i Montaner (1850-1923), Josep Puig i Cadafalch (1867-1957) and Antoni Gaudí i Cornet (1852-1926). During the 1890s, however, all the arts flourished - literature, theatre, music, painting, architecture and graphics.

By 1890 the printing industry in Catalonia had caught up with the rest of Europe. Printing equipment was mostly German because the foundry Bauersche Giesserei of Frankfurt had established a branch in Barcelona. The manufacture of inks and paper was modernised and the binding plants were brought up to date. One of the most avant-garde printing and publishing houses was L'Avenç, founded in 1891 and named after the leading Modernista literary magazine, both started by Jaume Massó i Torrents. As a result of all this modernisation and innovation Barcelona became one of the most important publishing centres in Europe during the next four decades; almost all books for the Spanish, Portuguese and Latin American markets were published there. After the Second World War Barcelona recovered much of this important market.

Modern developments in printing were paralleled in typographical design which nevertheless retained all its Catalan character. Modernista graphic artists designed illustrations for numerous books and journals, bookplates, posters, postcards and other printed ephemera.

Apel.les Mestres i Oños (1854-1936) was a prolific, influential artist, in addition to being a musician, playwright and writer and he was one of the first Spanish artists to understand and appreciate Japanese prints and Japonisme. Paris was a Mecca for Modernista artists and most of them managed to spend some time there. Among the first were Miquel Utrillo and Casas, two of the circle of artists who frequented Le Chat Noir in Montmartre. Current events in Paris were really the most important influence on most Modernista artists but others, such as Riquer, were also particularly interested by the work of Beardsley and others in London.

Alexandre de Riquer i Inglada (1856-1920), an extremely gifted poet, artist and designer, trained at the Llotja, then travelled to Rome, and visited Paris and London where he spent some time, returning to Spain in 1894. He was particularly interested in British book illustration of the 1890s and by Pre-Raphaelite art, encouraging enthusiasm for English Art Nouveau in Spain. When he returned to Barcelona from London for the second time he opened his own studio and soon became one of the most successful of the artistic literati in the city, a founder member of the Cercle Artistic de Sant Lluc. As early as 1890 he had a one-man exhibition at the Sala Parés, the first major commercial art gallery in the city. Later Riquer was the first artistic director of *Joventut*, artistic director of *Luz*, and a contributor to a number of other journals.

In 1896 a number of foreign posters, many of them French, were exhibited at the Sala Parés. The next year Riquer was commmssioned to design a poster for the IV Exposicion de Bellas Artes e Industrias Artisticas. Then the first Spanish poster competition was held, followed by numerous other exhibitions and competitions, at many of which Riquer won prizes, exhibiting successfully until his death. Santiago Rusiñol i Prats (1861-1931), the intellectual of the Modernista movement, studied at the Académie Gervex in Paris in 1885. On his return to Barcelona he took a studio, the original *Cau Ferrat* (den of iron), which became a great meeting-place for young artists. In 1892 this was replaced by a renovated old house in Sitges, convenient for the first (of five) *Festa modernista* during which there was an exhibition of paintings by Casas and Rusiñol, who contributed to a number of journals including the re-founded *L'Avenç* and *La Vanguardia*, for which he was the Paris correspondent.

Rusiñol returned to Paris in 1889 with Miquel Utrillo i Morlius (1862-1934) the critic who was one of the key figures of the Modernista movement, Enric Clarasó (1857-1941) the sculptor and Casas. Rusiñol exhibited with Casas and Clarasó jointly on several occasions.

Utrillo, Casas, Rusiñol and the cabaretier Père Romeu founded the café-concert Els Quatre Gats in June 1897, in a building designed by Puig i Cadafalch and modelled on Le Chat Noir in Montmartre. Very soon the café became a popular exhibition-hall, cabaret theatre, informal concert-hall and the home of a new children's puppet theatre Putxinel.lis. Rusiñol worked a great deal in the theatre, doing everything from writing plays to designing sets and costumes.

In 1899 Rusiñol showed a number of paintings of *Gardens of Spain* at L'Art Nouveau in Paris with success and he devoted almost all the rest of his working life to this subject, honoured at numerous exhibitions.

Ramón Casas i Carbó (1866-1932) studied with Carolus Duran in Paris from 1882 for some years. In 1889 his brother Joaquim Casas co-founded the publishing house L'Avenç which, with the review, was very influential and one of the main centres for the modernistes.

One of the co-founders of Els Quatre Gats, Casas had a number of successful exhibitions, including his attractive portrait drawings. The inner circle at the café published a magazine - *Quatre Gats* - in 1899, which was replaced by *Pèl & Ploma*. Casas was art director of both magazines and also of *Forma*, and designed many illustrations for these and other periodicals. Over the years he won many honours for both his commercial and fine art work, even being commissioned to paint a grand portrait of the king, in 1903. An imaginative critic, he was one of the first to appreciate the work of Pablo Picasso.

Riquer, Rusiñol, Adrià Gual i Queralt (1872-1944), Miquel Utrillo and Gaspar Camps i Junyent (1875-1942) all preferred a delicate, decorative artistic style, influenced by Mucha, Symbolism and British fantastic book illustration. They worked mainly for *Luz Joventut* and *Garba*.

The artists influenced by the realism of Toulouse-Lautrec and Steinlen, designing for *Quatre Gats*, *Pèl*

Ramón Casas: Anis del Mono

ANÍS DEL MONO

VICENTE BOSCH BADALONA ESPAÑA.

& Ploma and *Forma*, included Antoni Utrillo i Viadera (1867-1945), who founded the important lithographic company A. Utrillo y Rialp, Francisco de Cidó Navarro (1871-?) and, most importantly, Ramón Casas. From 1906 or so the extraordinary and exciting flowering of Modernisme was gradually superseded by Noucentisme, soon to be overtaken in its turn by modern art.

America

By the end of the nineteenth century America was no longer the Jeffersonian republic of farmers, but a continental nation; in many ways still the country of the founding fathers, but transmogrified by industrialisation, populous with immigrants of many national and ethnic origins, urbanised with great industrial centres, and modernised by the latest technical advances.

Morse had set up the first electric telegraph in 1844 between Washington and Baltimore, and in 1866 the first transatlantic cable was laid. In 1846 Cunard had established the first transatlantic steamship line. As in France, railroads were vital to the American economy; the first railroad, the Baltimore and Ohio, opened in 1830 and by shortly after 1910 there were 250,000 miles of railroad track. In the peak year of 1887 nearly 13,000 miles of track were laid.

Steamboats were navigated far inland, and meshing with the train system helped promote rapid economic growth. Between 1815 and 1914 about 35 million immigrants entered the United States from over twenty different cultural traditions and backgrounds. Because of its hardworking population and great resources, the United States was the world's leading industrial nation, producing more coal, iron, steel and raw cotton than the British Empire, more corn (the major field crop) than Russia; by 1910 the annual domestic output of petroleum exceeded 200 million barrels. By 1900 America's industrial output exceeded that of Great Britain and Germany combined. America grew rapidly between the end of the Civil War and the beginning of the First World War in production, consumption, and population.

118

American self-confidence and assurance was demonstrated in the Centennial Exposition of 1876 in Philadelphia and again in the World Columbian Exposition in Chicago in 1893 which was visited by about 28 million people. Many newly-prosperous

Americans wanted education and culture and were prepared to pay for them, from millionaires like Frick and Carnegie at one extreme to middle-class patrons in small Western towns at the other. The Centennial Exposition created a great deal of interest in things artistic; it reinforced the taste of rich Americans for French imports and it greatly encouraged the Arts and Crafts movement.

Many of the same factors were at work in America as in Europe to facilitate the emergence of a "new art": the growth of the popular press, the improvement of national and international communications, a general improvement in health, living standards, education and social reforms, and peace (with brief exceptions) both in Europe and the United States from 1871 to 1914.

The middle-classes were interested in new values and new products as well as in exotica, the taste for which had been much encouraged by the opening-up of Japan to the West. Through reading periodicals, the new patrons learned about the latest ideas and techniques. There was an ever-increasing number of architectural, art-historical and artistic books and magazines intended for professionals as well as the general public on both sides of the Atlantic. At this time there were more than 350 monthly magazines in New York alone. The publishers Scribner's carried the first American magazine advertising pages in 1887. During the 1890s the newspaper and bicycle industries particularly used posters for advertisement.

About this time Chicago, recovering from the fire of 1871, led the world in architectural innovations. Industrialists there, like so many other Americans, were receptive from the beginning to new ideas and commissioned revolutionary buildings as the city prospered and expanded. Louis Sullivan, who emerged as a great architect in Chicago, was one of the first modernists: his use of ornament was inspired by nature, remarkably individual and deeply expressive. In his designs he succeeded in harmonising objects with their decoration, both visually and functionally. Sullivan was influenced by the architecture of Frank Furness and, through him, by Owen Jones and by V. M. C. Ruprich-Robert, who was a colleague of Eugène Viollet-le-Duc at the Ecole Spéciale de Dessin for some years. The two volumes of Viollet-le-Duc's *Entretiens sur l'Architecture* (1863-72) were widely distributed

A. R. Glenny: *Women's Edition Buffalo Courier*, 1895, L of C

throughout Europe and America and, with his other writings, were extremely influential.

It seems possible by cross-fertilisation of ideas that some European designers were influenced in their turn by certain American advances in theory. Both H. H. Richardson, the architect, and John La Farge, artist and illustrator, were having a considerable effect on American art by about 1880, and some designs by Richardson and his associates early in the decade foreshadow later French work. It is of some interest that the first award to a non-French company at the Paris Exposition of 1867 was given to Tiffany and Co., of New York, headed by Charles Tiffany, the renowned jeweller and goldsmith.

The son of Charles Tiffany, Louis Comfort Tiffany (1848-1933) in 1879 founded the Louis C. Tiffany

119

A. W. Dow: *The Lotos*,
1896, L of C

Nouveau, Stephan Madsen says: "America ... made her contribution, in the work of Tiffany, but so far it has not been possible to determine whether the country played any part in the origins of this style". In *The Craftsman*, Professor A. D. F. Hamlin claimed that the earliest use of the term l'*Art Nouveau* occurred in 1893 in reference to work designed by Edward Chandler Moore (1827-91) and executed by Whiting, the silversmith, which was described as being in a style "derived from India" and "baptized 'Saracenic' by its creator" - i.e. Moore. Hamlin then refers to "the very new and very personal art of the Americans".

Henri Roujon, French Directeur des Beaux-Arts, strongly supported the design reform movement and with design reform in mind he asked Siegfried Bing, who had visited the United States in 1894, to describe

Company of Associated Artists, an interior design and furnishing company (later merged with the Tiffany Glass Company) which produced among other things much stained glass, then very popular in the United States. Tiffany's art, it is generally agreed, had three major sources: the stylised forms of Japanese art; the symmetry and colours of Islamic art, as illustrated by Owen Jones; and naturalistic plant forms derived from his interest in American flora and fauna and from the illustrations in Christopher Dresser's books as well. His work was influenced by designs by Voysey and Baillie Scott which were published in *The Studio* and perhaps by those of Colonna (a former employee) if, as is quite possible, he was given a copy of Colonna's *Essay on Broom Corn* (1887).

Speaking of possible American sources of Art

F. Lundborg: *The Lark*,
1895, L of C

120

M. Knowles: *The Lotus*, 1896, L of C

W. H. Bradley: *The Chap Book*, 1895 Va.

directing artists, themselves united by a common current of ideas.'"

The only major Art Nouveau residence Bing saw in America was Louis Tiffany's own country house Laurelton Hall in Oyster Bay, Long Island, designed by Robert Pryor. The Tiffany mansion on Madison Avenue in New York, designed by Stanford White, had some Art Nouveau design features, as did various other houses, but Laurelton Hall was the most important.

While praising the new art in America, Bing also commended the American ability to organise the industrial process to make products of high artistic quality. A successful union of labour and industrial processes was achieved partly he thought because Americans expected thereby to reach a large clientèle and so to succeed both commercially and artistically. Bing insisted however that artists must be certain to establish their artistic goals before letting the manufacturing processes take over, and that the aim

his impressions of American industrial arts. The result was an extremely interesting short book called La Culture *Artistique en Amérique* in which Bing praised America's painting, sculpture, architecture, industrial and decorative arts. Bing was particularly impressed by the work of Edward Moore and Louis Tiffany and by Richardson's architecture. Moore, a brilliant designer and silversmith, had been artistic director of Tiffany and Co. since 1868. Bing said that Moore was "one of the first to comprehend the real value of the art treasures emerging from the Orient". Like Tiffany he collected Oriental art. In his book Bing described Tiffany's studios as "a vast central workshop that would consolidate under one roof an army of craftsmen representing every relevant technique: glass-makers, embroiderers and weavers, casemakers and carvers, gilders, jewellers, cabinet makers - all working to give shape to the carefully planned concepts of a group of

121

W. H. Bradley: *The Chap Book* (September), 1895. L of C

122

W. H. Bradley: *Fringilla*,
by R. D. Blackmore,
1895. L of C

strangest aberrations to the most exquisite creations"
and he argued that the main reason for the
progressiveness of the arts in the United States was the
lack of a strong tradition, which sometimes can be
retrogressive and foster imitations. Although as yet he
found no unity of direction, theory or style he did see
"many striving for success, wealth, fame and artistic
quality". Bing's book was serialised in France and
earned him considerable esteem in the United States
where it was greatly appreciated.

Later Bing commissioned Tiffany to execute
stained-glass windows designed by Denis, Ibels,
Ranson, Sérusier, Vallotton, Vuillard, Toulouse-
Lautrec and Grasset. The windows (few of which
survive) were shown in Paris at the Société Nationale
des Beaux-Arts in 1895 before most of them were
exhibited at Bing's Salon de l'Art Nouveau at the end
of that year. Tiffany, himself always receptive to new
ideas, brought new influences from Europe to America
and publicised American art and design in Europe.

Oscar Wilde's dictum that "all the arts are fine arts
and all the arts are decorative arts" is apt when applied
to Tiffany's work. Wilde toured the United States
lecturing in 1882 spreading the Aesthetic message; he
stressed "modernity" and "individualism of
expression", two vital elements of Art Nouveau.

New museums and increasing travel abroad
encouraged great interest in the arts among influential
Americans, one sign of which was the formation of
many Women's Clubs to sponsor culture. During the
1880s and 1890s numerous art groups and societies
were founded with an enthusiasm fuelled by new art
magazines. A flood of such publications provided
commissions for numerous graphic artists, many of
whom worked in the popular Art Nouveau style,

Among the artistic origins of the new graphic style,
English and Japanese influences were particularly
important. William Morris' influence was strong on
American Art Nouveau graphic arts; especially the
books of the Kelmscott Press insofar as they embodied
the ideas and philosophy of Morris and Company.
Another influential English artist Walter Crane won a
number of prizes at the Centennial Exposition (1876)
and during the next decade his illustrated children's
books became very popular. Eugène Grasset was given
the commission for the November 1882 cover of *Frank
Leslie's Illustrated Newspaper;* his work was much

was to use mechanisation to produce applied art.

Bing observed that for every kind of American
product all levels of quality were to be found from "the

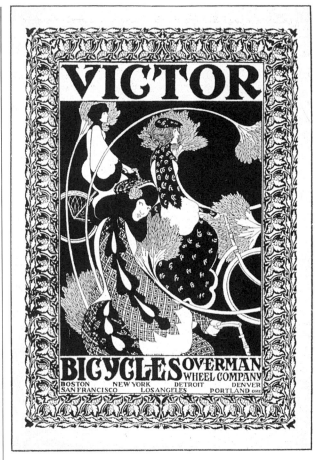

began to meet other designers, including Frederic W. Goudy, the typographer, whom he befriended. In 1890 Bradley designed a typeface which the American Type Founders Company later bought and named after him. The year of the Chicago World's Fair, at which he exhibited, Bradley's studio was in the Monadnock building; he received many commissions related to the fair, including the Exposition souvenir booklet of Harriet Monroe's poem *The Columbian Ode*. At this time he designed the covers of a trade journal The *Inland Printer*, the first journal to change its cover with each issue.

When a "poster craze" swept the country during the 1890s, the only American poster designs at first available were Edward Penfield's for *Harper's Monthly* and Bradley's for *The Chap Book*. *The Chap Book* was the house journal of the printing and publishing firm Stone and Kimball of Chicago and Cambridge, Massachusetts. Most of the posters exhibited then were by French artists, notably Grasset, who was particularly popular with Americans, Chéret and Toulouse-Lautrec, although some were by German and English

appreciated in America, particularly following the publication of *Histoire des quatre fils Aymon*, a landmark in the history of book illustration.

The "Dean of American Typographers" charmingly narrates his own life, partly using the historical present, in his autobiography *Will Bradley His Chap Book* describing "his graphic arts adventures: as boy printer in Ishpeming; art student in Chicago; designer, printer and publisher at the Wayside Press; the years as art director in periodical publishing, and the interludes of stage, cinema and authorship."

Befriended by a visiting artist in Ishpeming, Michigan, Bradley (1868-1962) reached Chicago eventually, after a thorough training as a jobbing printer. At nineteen he started designing for a large commercial printing firm, was involved with the use of the first halftones engraved and printed in that city and gained more and more useful experience. Soon he

artists. Bradley designed a poster for *The Masqueraders* by Henry Arthur Jones which, he said, "was probably the first *signed* theatrical poster produced by any American lithographer".

At the Players' Theatre in New York Bradley saw showbills set in Caslon which he said influenced all his "future work in the field of typography". He was excited by the "Colonial typography" used in early American printing which he felt showed a long-lost, joyous spontaneity, Emery Walker and William Morris' Kelmscott Press books, especially the *Chaucer*, inspired the private press movement, including the Wayside Press, which, in their turn, revitalised the Commercial press. In Bradley's work one can see unity in the employment of type, ink and paper throughout, and the use of the opening as the basic unit of design. After moving to Geneva, Illinois he designed for a wide variety of books, newspapers, and magazines.

V. L. George: *The Bostonian*, 1895, L of C

E. Penfield: *Harper's*
1896, L of C

E. B. Bird: *The Poster*, 1896, L of C

attention nationally by his use of the Caslon face.

His business was successful but Bradley was overwhelmed by the practical complications of expansion and it was merged with the University Press in Cambridge. After Bradley had recovered from the illness caused by the strain, Edward Bok of the *Ladies' Home Journal* commissioned eight full pages of house interiors from him, which were influenced by Charles Rennie Mackintosh's designs. A series of house plans followed. During these years Bradley designed several covers for *Collier's Weekly* and in 1904 a new series of *Chap Books* started. Bradley's designs were widely admired and a number of artists were strongly influenced by his work, including F.Y. Long who designed many illustrations in a romantic style with flowing, curvy lines. In 1907 Bradley became art editor of *Collier's*, subsequently introducing new techniques in make-up, art direction and typography. Between 1880 and 1904 the total amount of money spent on

Emboldened by this success, Bradley went to Boston, settled in Springfield, Massachusetts, and started the Wayside Press at the Sign of the Dandelion. Inspired by the Vale Press books of Charles Ricketts and by Aubrey Beardsley's illustrations in the *Yellow Book* as well as by Elihu Vedder's *Rubáiyat of Omar Khayyám* (1884), Bradley planned to publish a few personally designed and executed brochures and booklets as well as a magazine. In the event the first publication of the Wayside Press was a Strathmore deckle-edge sample book. This was so successful that it brought in a great deal of business. In May 1896 Bradley published *Bradley: His Book* Volume one, Number one (subscription price one dollar a year). The Book was planned as an art and literary magazine and also as "a technical journal for those engaged in the art of printing". In 1896 Bradley exhibited at the first show of the Boston Arts and Crafts Society, attracting much

E. Penfield: *Harper's*, 1892, L of C

128

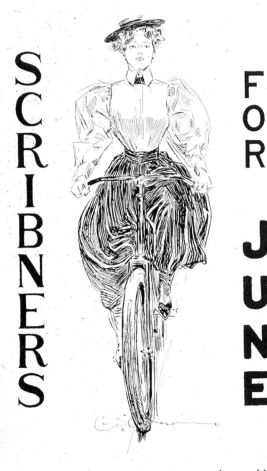

further new principles of illustration and typographical layout. Among many other awards, he received the coveted Gold Medal of the American Institute of Graphic Arts in 1954.

Bradley's artistic principles were directness and simplicity, unity and spontaneity. Influences on his work included: the Vienna Secession, Japanese woodcuts, the Arts and Crafts Movement, Burne-Jones, Mackintosh, Grasset, Ricketts, and Laurence Housman as well as Beardsley, who was the most important. However, as A. H. McQuilkin, editor of The Inland Printer, said: "He has never been imitative." From the first Bradley used line positively and in a very versatile way with a remarkable feeling for black and white space; he said that every compositor should have in his shop a label reading "Do with me as little as you can, not as much". As Walter Dorwin Teague's 1954 introduction to *Will Bradley His Chap Book* puts it: "There were derivative traces in Bradley's early work - and whose hasn't? - but when he hit his stride it wasn't Europe's leadership he followed. He

C. D. Gibson: *Scribners,* 1895, L of C

advertising each year in America more than trebled to 140 million dollars and the rôle of the art editor became vital to the process of selling and marketing.

From 1910 to 1915 Bradley was art editor of *Good Housekeeping, Metropolitan, Success, Pearson's,* and the *National Post* and, among other commissions, wrote the series of tales which were published later as the *Wonderbox Stories.* During his long and varied career in several media, he became art director for the Hearst companies, commissioning work from Dulac, Rackham and Brangwyn, among others,

Fascinated by type all his life, early in the 1890s Bradley was experimenting with asymmetric designs, exploring new modes of expression of ideas on paper with type and ink. His designs were admired in Europe by later designers like the great typographer Jan Tschichold. During the 1920s Bradley developed

J. C. Leyendecker: *The Chap Book,* 189-, L of C

129

E. Penfield: *Harper's*,
1895, L of C

E. Reed: *The New
Illustrated Magazine*, 189
L of C

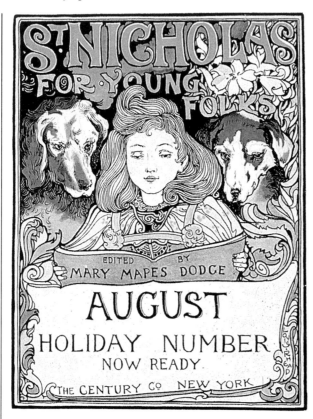

L. Rhead: *St. Nicholas*, 1894, L of C

discovered American colonial typography, bold and free, and from that springboard he took off into a career of non-archaic, non-repetitive, exuberant and exhilarating design. In its way it was as American as the Declaration of Independence. In this field we have never had any more indigenous art than Bradley's."

In *Bradley: His Book* (No.1) the designer wrote an article on Edward Penfield (1866-1925) in which he praised him as a true artist and rightly described him as a "master" who designed posters "wholly as a medium of expression peculiarly adapted to his own line of thought" not just to "satisfy the craze for collecting them". Bradley also said about him that "in methods of reproduction, that difficult point to which so few give even a passing thought, he is a past master", which from Bradley is praise indeed.

Edward Penfield, illustrator, painter, designer and author, was born in Brooklyn in 1866. Trained at the Art Students' League he began his career with Harper & Brothers, and was the illustrator for Harper publications becoming art editor from 1890 to 1901,

J. Sloan: *The Echo*, 1895, L of C

132

M. Parrish: *Scribners*,
1897, L of C

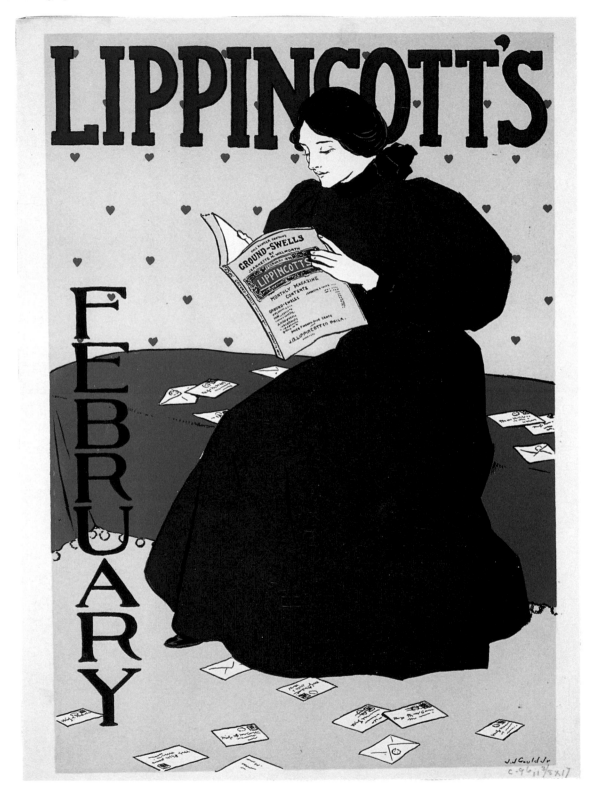

W. L. Carqueville:
Lippincott's, 189-, L of C
134

L. Rhead: *The Century*,
1894, L of C

during the "Golden Age" of magazine publishing. Compared to newspapers, magazines had been slow to accept advertising, but then found doing so well worth their while as innovations in photographic reproduction and printing lowered costs and encouraged greater use of illustrations. The second-class mail rate established by the Postal Act of 1879 also resulted in lower subscription rates. Penfield was one of the most popular artists of the time; his magazine covers were outstanding, but he is best known for his elegant, attractive posters in which he used definite lines, little detail and large flat areas of colour, fully appreciating the technical advances made in colour lithography. As he himself wrote: "I think the American Poster has opened a new school whose aim is simplicity and good composition." Scribner's published two of his books *Holland Sketches* and *Spanish Sketches*. Penfield later taught at the Art Students' League and through his students, his posters and his magazine work had, as Bradley said, a "profound effect on American illustration".

Louis Rhead (1857-1926), one of three brothers, was born in England and studied art in Paris and London, where his bookbinding designs were much admired. He emigrated to America in 1883 at the invitation of the Appleton Publishing Company of New York, living first in Brooklyn and then further out on Long Island. Rhead was a successful ceramic designer, portrait painter, poster designer, lithographer, watercolour artist and illustrator in black-and-white. In the United States he is probably best known for the colour covers and posters he designed for *Harper's*, *The Century*, *The Sun*, *The Journal*, *St.Nicholas* and other periodicals. From 1891 to 1894 he was working and studying in Europe where he came to know Grasset and was much influenced by his work. In 1895 he had a large one-man show at the Wunderlich Gallery in New York which established his reputation in America, further consolidated by the Gold Medal he won soon afterwards at the International Poster Exhibition in Boston. In 1896 he had a solo exhibition of his posters in London and in 1897 he had a one-man poster exhibition at the Salon des Cent in Paris, being the only American to do so in either city. In *La Plume* a French critic said: "These designs modestly catalogued as advertising posters are really magnificent frescoes constituting the most

W. H. Bradley: *The Modern Poster*, 1895, L of C

charming mural decoration possible." In 1904 Rhead won a Gold Medal at the St.Louis Exposition for his oil and watercolour work. In his posters Rhead demonstrated an original feeling for colour and the intense colour combinations he used so successfully.

Maxfield Parrish (1870-1966) was the son of a painter and etcher, Stephen Parrish. He began by studying architecture but went on to the Pennsylvania Academy of Fine Arts later, like so many others, studying with Howard Pyle (1853-1911), the well-known illustrator. In 1896 Parrish and Robert Vonnoh organised a poster exhibition at the Academy for which Parrish designed both the poster and the catalogue

cover. During the same year he received two awards: second prize in *The Century* poster contest and first prize in the Pope Manufacturing Company's Columbia bicycle poster competition. Like Pyle's, many of Parrish's illustrations were romantic, escapist and imaginary; they were technically very accomplished but conventional compared to those by Bradley. Parrish's prints, posters and magazine covers were very successful.

First prize in *The Century* poster competition was won by Joseph Christian Leyendecker (1874-1951) who went to Paris the same year to continue his studies at the Académie Julian. Leyendecker was born in Germany and emigrated to America when he was eight years old; he started work for a Chicago printing firm in 1891 and attended evening classes at the Art Institute. Winning The Century prize brought him numerous commissions. In 1899, the year of his first cover (of over 300) for *The Saturday Evening Post*, he moved to New York where he shared a studio with his younger brother, Frank X. Leyendecker (1877-1924), also an illustrator, whose work was attractive and competent but lacked the verve and assurance of his older brother's designs.

Various other artists can be described as having worked in an Art Nouveau style, including Edwin A. Abbey (1852-1911). Most of Abbey's work is in a robust, realistic style but his drawings and the unsigned binding for *Selections from the Hesperides* and *Noble Numbers of Robert Herrick* published in New York in 1882 show the influence of Art Nouveau interestingly early. Elisha Brown Bird (1867-1943) was an architect, illustrator, artist and cartoonist who designed posters and illustrations for *The Inland Printer, St. Nicholas and The Chap Book*, as well as for many books.

Nothing is known about Ethel Reed's career after she went to Ireland for a rest following a voyage to Europe in May 1896 "to study in the broad school of life". Reed (1874-after 1900) was largely self-taught which makes the skill and style of her book illustrations and posters all the more remarkable; her poster designs demonstrate an understanding of the principles that lie behind the original designs of Bradley, Penfield and Rhead. Reed was the best-known woman artist during the "poster craze" in America; the originality of her style was praised by Bradley who said that her work was "controlled in a measure, as most poster makers are, by French or Japanese methods of treatment".

James McNeill Whistler was one of the first Western artists to take an informed and serious interest in Oriental art, as demonstrated by his paintings, books and designs. Whistler's magnificent designs for the Peacock Room (now in the Freer Gallery, Washington) confirmed peacocks as one of the most popular themes for Art Nouveau artists, exemplified in America by well-known artists like Bradley and Rhead and also by illustrators like Sarah S. Stilwell Weber. A student of Howard Pyle's at the Drexel Institute in Philadelphia and also at Chadds Ford, Weber worked for various magazines including St. Nicholas, illustrating numerous children's books in an Eastern-inspired, imaginative style.

John Sloan, famous as a member of the "Ashcan School" of painters, moved to New York from Philadelphia in 1904. During the previous fifteen years or so, he worked for several Philadelphia newspapers as an illustrator and designed a number of posters in a very striking expressively graphic style clearly influenced by Japanese woodcuts.

Another artist whose style was striking and expressive was William L. Carqueville (1871-1946), sometimes unfairly described as an imitator of Penfield's designs primarily because his series of posters for *Lippincott's* were in competition with the *Harper's* series. In his posters, however, Carqueville demonstrates his understanding of contemporary work on the Continent and also of the possibilities inherent in the lithographic process; he trained in the family firm of Shober and Carqueville, printers in Chicago. After studying in Paris during 1896 he returned to Chicago and worked as a freelance illustrator.

After the turn of the century, fashions changed and there was a reaction against the Art Nouveau style in favour of realistic and "Colonial American" designs in illustration. The posters of the 1890s were succeeded by the even more successful advertising campaigns of the twentieth century. The interesting ideas of Tiffany and his confrères were superseded by the "sensible, honest, sturdy" designs of Gustav Stickley, and the attractive, imaginative, artistic magazines were replaced by *The Philistine*.

Selected Bibliography

The literature on Art Nouveau is extensive; earlier references may be found in James Grady's bibligraphy. Almost all the books in the following list contain further references.

Amaya, M. *Art Noveau* revised ed. London 1975

American Art Posters of the 1890s exhibition New York 1987

Bairati, E., Bossaglia, R., Rosci, M. *Italia Liberty* Milan 1970

Borisova, H. A., Sternine, G. *Art Nouveau Russe* Paris 1987

Borsi, F. Godoli, E. *Paris 1900* New York 1977

Ciricer Pellicer, A., Gomis, J. *Barcelona 1900* Barcelona 1967

Dreams of a Summer Night exhibition London 1986

Fanelli, G., Godoli, E. *Art Nouveau Postcards* London 1987

Gans, L. *Nieuwe Kunst. De Nederlandse Bijdrage tot de Art Nouveau* Utrecht 1960

Grady, J. "Bibliography of Art Nouveau" *Journal of Society of Architectural Historians* XIV May 1955 pp.18-27

Gray, C. *The Russian Experiment in Art 1863-1922* revised ed. New York 1986

Howarth, T. C. *R. Mackintosh and the Modern Movement* second ed. London1977

Johnson, D. C. *American Art Nouveau* New York 1979

Madsen, T. S. *Sources of Art Nouveau* second ed. New York 1975

Marx, C. Roger *Les Maîtres de l'Affich* 5 vols. Paris 1896-1900

Selz, P., Constantine, M.,eds. *Art Nouveau* revised ed. New York 1975

Taylor, J. R. *The Art Nouveau Book in Britain* London 1966

Varnedoe, K. *Vienna 1900: art, architecture and design* New York 1986

Vergo, P. *Art in Vienna, 1898-1918* London 1975

Wallis, M. *Secesja* Warsaw 1967

Weisberg, G. P. *Art Nouveau Bing: Paris Style 1900* New York 1986

Selected Contemporary Periodicals

Apollon St. Petersburg 1909-17 (1918)

Art and Decoration New York 1885-6

L'Art Décoratif Paris 1898-1914

L'Arte decorativa moderna Turin 1902

Art Italiana Decorativa ed Industriale Rome 1890-1914

Art et Décoration Paris 1897-

Art et Industrie Paris 1909-14

L'Art et les Artistes Paris 1905-39

Artistic Japan London 1889-91

L'Art Moderne Brussels 1881-1914

The Art Record London 1901-2

L'Avenç Barcelona 1881-4, 1889-1893

Bouw en Siekunst Amsterdam/Haarlem 1897-1904

Bradley: His Book Springfield, Mass. 1896-97

Zeitschrift fur Bucherfreunde Bielefeld/Leipzig 1897-192

Catalonia Barcelona 1898

Catalonia Artística Barcelona 1900-5

The Chap Book Chicago 1894-98

Le Chat Noir Paris 1882-1895

Chimera Warsaw 1901-7

Le Courrier FrançaisParis 1886-94

The Craftsman Eastwood, New York 1901-16

Dekorative Kunst Munich 1897-1929

Dekorative Vorbilder Stuggart 1889-1929

Deutsche Kunst und Dekoration Darmstadt 1897-1934

The Dial London 1889-97

The Echo Chicago 1895-98

Emporium Bergamo 1895-1964

L'Estampe et l'Affiche Paris 1897-99

L'Estampe Moderne Paris 1897-1899

The Evergreen Edinburgh/London 1895-97

Forma Barcelona 1899-1907

Forms and Fantasies Chicago 1898-99

Garba Barcelona 1905-6

Il giovane artista moderno Turin 1902

Die Graphischen Dunste Vienna 1879-

Handicrafts Boston 1902-

The Hobby Horse London 1884(no.1),1886-92, 1893-4

House and Garden Philadelphia 1901-

House Beautiful Chicago 1896-

Illustrierte kunstgewerbliche Zeitschrift fur Innen-Dekoration, Ausschmuckung und Einrichtung der Wohnraume Darmstadt 1889-

L'Image Paris 1896-7

The Inland Printer Chicago 1887-
Die Insel Berlin 1899-1901/Leipzig 1902
Das Interieur Vienna 1900
Interior Decorator Chicago 1891-4
L'Italia che ride Bologna 1900
Le Japon Artistique Paris 1888-91
Joventut Barcelona 1900-6
Jugend Munich 1896-1933
The Knight Errant Boston 1892-3
Knudozhestvennoye Sokrovische Rossii St. Petersburg
    1901-7
Kunst Copenhagen 1899-1905
Die Kunst Munich 1897-1945
Kunst und Dekoration Darmstadt 1897
Kunst und Kunsthandwerk Vienna 1898-1921
Kunst und Kunsthandwerk Stuttgart 1902-
Ladies' Home Journal New York 1901-
The Lark San Francisco 1895-6
La Libre Esthètique Brussels 1894-1914
Lotos Kansas City, Mo. 1896
Luz Barcelona 1897-8
The Magazine of Art London 1878-1904
Magyar Iparmuveszet Budapest 1897-1909
Les Maîtres de l'Affiche Paris 1896-1900
Mintalopek Budapest 1895-1905
Mir Iskusstva St. Petersburg 1898-1904
Der Moderne Stil Stuttgart 1899-1905
Novi put St. Petersburg 1906-7
Novissima Milan/Rome 1900-
The Pageant London 1896-7
Pan Berlin 1895-1900
Pèl & Ploma successor to Quatre Gats 1899-1903
The Penrose Annual London 1895-
The Philistine Aurora, N.Y. 1895-1916
Das Plakat Berlin 1910-21
La Plume Paris 1899-1914
The Poster New York 1896
The Poster London 1898-1901
Poster Lore Kansas City, Mo. 1896
Quatre Gats Barcelona 1899
La Renaixença Barcelona 1871-1905
Revue des Arts Décoratifs Paris 1880-1902
La Revue Blanche Paris 1891-1903
Revue Wagnérienne Paris 1885-88
Le Rire Paris 1894-1914
The Savoy London 1896
Simplicissimus Munich 1896-1967

Stariye godi St. Petersburg 1907-16
The Studio London 1893-
La Vanguardia Barcelona 1889-93
Van Nu en Straks Brussels/Antwerp 1893-1901
*Ver Sacrum: Mitteilungen der Vereinigung bildender
Kunstler Osterreichs I-IV* Vienna 1898-1903
Vesi Moscow 1904-9
The Yellow Book London 1894-97
Zolotoïe Rouno Moscow 1906-9 (1910)

Museums

Musée Toulouse-Lautrec et Galerie d'Art Moderne,
    Albi
Stedelijk Museum, Amsterdam
Museo de Arte de Cataluña, Barcelona
Museo de Arte Moderno, Barcelona
Rasmus Meyers Samlinger, Bergen
Stiftelsen Stenersens Samling, Bergen
Vestlandske Kunstindustrimuseum, Bergen
Brücke-Museum, Berlin
Neue Nationalgalerie, Berlin
National-Galerie, East Berlin
Kunstmuseum, Berne
Kunsthalle, Bielefeld
Museum of Fine Arts, Boston
Kunsthalle Bremen, Bremen
Museum and Art Gallery, Brighton
Musées Royaux des Beaux -Arts, Brussels
Magyar Nemzeti Galeria, Budapest
Busch-Reisinger Museum, Cambridge
Art Institute of Chicago, Chicago
Det Danske Kunstindustrimuseum, Copenhagen
Hessisches Landemuseum, Darmstadt
Kunstmuseum, Düsseldorf
National Gallery of Scotland, Edinburgh
Museum Folkwang, Essen
Glasgow Art Gallery and Museum, Glasgow
Hunterian Art Gallery, Glasgow
Goteborgs Konstmuseum, Goteborg
Museum für Kunst und Gewerbe, Hamburg
Ateneumin Taidemuseo, Helsinki
Russian State Museum, Lenigrad
Musée des Beaux -Arts, Liège
Neue Galerie der Stadt Linz Wolfgang-Gurlitt-
    Museum, Linz
Victoria and Albert Musuem, London
William Morris Gallery, Walthamstow, London
Behnhaus, Lübeck
Malmo Museum, Malmo
Manchester City Art Gallery, Manchester
Galleria d'Arte Moderna, Milan
Tretyakov Gallery, Moscow
Neue Pinakothek/ Staatsgalerie Moderner Kunst,
    Munich
Stuck-Jugendstil-Verein e.V. Museumn Stuck Villa
    Munich

Musée des Beaux-Arts, Nancy
Musée Corbin, Nancy
Jane Voorhees Zimmerli Art Museum, Rutgers
    University, New Brunswick
Cooper-Hewitt Museum, New York
Metropolitan Museum of Art, New York
Museum of Modern Art, New York
New York Public Library, New York
Musée des Beaux-Arts Jules Chéret, Nice
Sainsbury Centre, Norwich
Munch-Museet, Oslo
Nasjonalgalleriet, Oslo
Rijksmuseum Kröller Müller, Otterlo
Musée des Arts Décoratifs, Paris
Musée National d'Art Moderne, Paris
Musée d'Orsay, Paris
Musée de la Publicitè et de l'Affiche, Paris
Museum of Fine Art, Philadelphia
Pennsylvania Academy of Fine Art, Philadelphia
Národni Galerie v Praze, Prague
Virginia Museum of Art, Richmond, Virginia
Galleria Nazionale d'Arte Moderna, Rome
Huntingdon Library, San Marino, California
Nolde-Museum, Seebnll
Skagens Museum, Skagen
Moderna Museet, Stockholm
Nordiska Museet, Stockholm
Waldemarsudde, Stockholm
Galleria d'Arte Moderna, Turin
Turku Taidemuseo, Turku
Galleria d'Arte Moderna, Venice
Historisches Museum der Stadt Wien, Vienna
Museum Moderner Kunst, Vienna
Österreichische Galerie des 19. and 20.
    Jahrhunderts, Vienna
Österreichische Museum für Angewandte Kunst,
    Vienna
Muzeum Narodow, Warsaw
Freer Gallery of Art, Washington, D.C.
Library of Congress, Washington, D.C.
National Gallery of Art, Washington, D.C.
Phillips collection, Washington, D.C.
Von der Heydt-Museum, Wuppertal
Kunstgewerbermuseum, Zürich
Kunsthaus, Zürich

Selected Exhibitions

1851 Great Exhibition - London
1855 Paris
1862 London
1867 Paris
1871-4 London
1873 Vienna World Exposition
1876 Philadelphia Centennial Exposition
1876 Union Centrale des Beaux-Arts - Paris
1878 Paris
1886 Liverpool
1886 Barcelona
1888 Arts and Crafts Exhibition Society - London
1888 Glasgow International Exhibition
1889 Paris
1893 Chicago World Columbian Exposition
1894 Nancy
1894 Atnwerp
1894 San Francisco
1894 Madrid
1894 Lyon
1895 Les Vingt - Brussels
1896 Salon de la Libre Esthétique - Brussels
1896 Salon de l'Art Nouveau - Paris
1897 Art and Industry Stockholm
1897 Brussels-Tervueren
1897 St Petersburg
1898 Secession I and II - Vienna
1899 Salon de la Libre Esthétique - Brussels
1899 Secession III, IV and V - Vienna
1899 Collection of S. Bing, Grafton Gallery, London
1899 Secession - Munich
1899 Deutsche Kunstaustellung - Dresden
1900 Secession VI, VII and VIII - Vienna
1900 Paris Exposition Universelle
1900 Salon de la Libre Esthétique - Brussels
1900 Krefeld
1901 Glasgow
1901 Dresden
1901 Secession, IX, X, XI and XII - Vienna
1901 Darmstadt
1902 Turin
1902 Secession XIII, XIV and XV - Vienna
1902 Rome
1903 Salon de la Libre Esthétique - Brussels
1903 Secession XVI, XVII and XVIII

1904 Darmstadt
1904 Secession XIX and XX - Vienna
1904 St. Louis
1904 Ecole de Nancy - Paris
1905 Liège
1905 Secession XXI, XXII, XXIII and XXIV Vienna
1906 Dresden
1906 Secession XXV, XXVI and XXVII - Vienna
1906 Milan
1906 Exhibition of Russian Art - Paris
1907 Secession XXVIII and XXIX - Vienna
1907 Irish International Exhibition
1908 Franco-British Exhibition - London
1908 Secession XXX and XXXI - Vienna
1909 Stockholm
1910 Brussels
1911 Rome, Turin and Palermo
1912 Arts and Crafts - London
1913 Ghent
1913 Armory Show - New York
1914 Baltic Exhibition Malmö

Index

Page numbers in italic refer to the illustrations

Abbey, Edwin A 138
Adler, Friedrich 68
Alliance Provinciale des Artistes (Ecole de Nancy) 9
Amsterdamse Kunstkring 49
Andreev, Nikolai 106
Architecture: America 119; Austria-Hungary 87, 89; Belgium 57; France 8; Germany 71, 83; Great Britain 83; Italy 43-4; Netherlands 51; Russia 104
Arts and Crafts movement 28-31, 36, 51, 53, 57, 90, 110, 111, 115
Ashbee, Charles Robert 30, 91
Auriol, Georges (Jean-Georges Huyot) 20

Bacher, Rudolf 89
Baillie Scott, Mackay Hugh *81*, 83, 120
Bakst, Léon (Lev Rosenberg) 105, 106
Ballerio, Osvaldo 43
Basile, Ernesto 45
Bauhaus 68, 71
Beardsley, Aubrey 13, 32-7, *32-5*, 36-8, 42, 49, 68, 101, 102, 105, 116, 128
Beggarstaff Brothers (Sir William Nicholson and James Pryde) 34-5, 36, *36-7*, 42, 77
Behrens, Peter 65, 67, 70-1, 73, 83
Bell, Robert Anning 32
Beltrami, Giovanni 43
Benois, Alexander 105
Berchmans, Emile 65
Bergh, Richard 111
Berlage, Hendrik Petrus 51
Berlin Secession 65, 67, 77, 88, 109
Berthon, Paul Emile 12, 22-3
Besnard, Paul 67
Bierbaum, Otto Julius 68
Bilbine, Ivan 106
Bilek, Frantisek 96
Bindesboll, Thorvald 112
Bing, Siegfried 7, 8-10, 14, 31, 53, 57, 68, 121-3
Bird, Elisha Brown *128*, 138
Birlé, Charles 105
Biró, Mihály 94
Bistolfi, Leonardo 45
Blake, William 30, 43, 49
Blaue Reiter group 106
Boccioni, Umberto 45
Boldini, Giovanni 45
Bonnard, Pierre 12, 15, 17-18, *18*, 41, 46
Bonnat, Léon 24, 109
book design *see* typography and book design
book illustration: Austria-Hungary 95; France 19-20; Great Britain 28, 32-4, 116; Italy 45
Borisov-Musatov, Victor 106
Bosselt, Rudolf 83
Boulanger, Henri *see* Gray, Henry

Bradley, W H *121-3*, 124-32, *124-5*, *136*
Brandes, Georg 110
Brangwyn, Frank 31, *31*, 123
Breitner, George H 49
Bukowski, Jan 100
Burck, Paul 83
Burne-Jones, Edward 28, 30, 32, 33, 68, 102
Burns, Robert 38
Buszek, Antoni 102

Cachet, C A Lion 51, *52*
Cambellotti, Duilio 45
Camps i Junyent, Gaspar 117
Cappiello, Leonetto 46, *46*
Carqueville, William L *134*, 138
Carrière, Eugène 67
Casas i Carbó, Ramón *113*, 116-17, *117*
Casorati, Felice 45
Cauchie, Paul 57
Cézanne, Paul 53
Chéret, Jules, 10-14, *11-13*, 17, 20, 28, 41, 43, 46, 94, 121
Chini, Galileo 45
Christiansen, Hans *75*, 80
Cidó Navarro, Francisco 117
Ciurlionis, Mikolojus 106
Clarasó, Enric 117
Clarke, Henry Patrick 39
classical influences: Great Britain 33; Italy 45; Russia 104
Comencini, G B 44
Cometti, G 45
Coppedè, Gino 44
Cordier, Eugène 80
Corinth, Lovis 67
Costa, Nino 43
Craig, Edward Gordon 35
Crane, Walter 20, 29-32, *30*, 32, 41
Crespin, Adolphe 56, *56*, 60
Czajkowski, Jozef 100
Czech Secession 97
Czeschka, Karl 93
Cziurlonis, Mikolojus Konstantinas 102

d'Aronco, Raimondo 44
Daum brothers 9
Daumier, Honoré 25
Davidson, George Dutch 38
Day, Lewis 30
Debicki, Stanislaw 102
de Chavannes, Puvis 88, 96, 104
de Feure, Georges (George Joseph van Sluijters) 13-14, *14*
Degas, Edgar 25
de Karolis, Adolfo 44, 45
Dekorative Kunst 67, 68, 70
Denis, Maurice 14-16, *15-16*, 49, 57, 96, 112
de Requier, Alexandre *114-5*
De Stijl 51
Deutsche Werkstätten 70
Deutscher Werkbund 68, 70, 83

Diaghilev, Sergei Pavlovich 105
Die Elf 67
Die Scholle 77
Diez, Julius 80, *82*
Dijsselhof, G W 31, 51
Divéky, Jozsef 94
Dobbelmann, J 53
Dobuzhinsky, Mstislav 105
Domènech i Montaner, Lluis 116
Donnay, Auguste *63*, 65
Doré, Gustave 18, 24
Dow, A W *120*
Dudovich, Marcello 43
Dufrène, Maurice 10
Duncan, John 38
Düsseldorfer Kunstgewerbeschule 71
Duyck, Edouard 56, 64

Eckmann, Otto 67, *70*, 71-2, *73*
Edelfelt, Albert 110
embroidery: Germany 68
Endell, August 68-70
Endell, Fritz 70
Ensor, James 49, *61*, 64
Erler, Fritz 101
Evenepoel, Henri 60
Expressionists 64, 96, 102

Falus, Elek 94
fantasy: Great Britain 117; Poland 101
Faragó, Géza 94
Fauves 88
Fenoglio, Pietro 44
Filosofov, Dmitri 105
Finch, Willy 110
Fjaestad, Gustaf 111
Földes, Imre 95
Follot, Paul 10, 22
"Four" *see* "The Four"
French, Annie 38
Frycz, Karol 100
furniture and interiors: Belgium 57; Germany 70; Great Britain 36-7; Italy 45

Gallé, Emile 9
Gallen-Kallela, Akseli (Axel Gallén) 109-11
garden cities: Germany 70
Gaudí i Cornet, Antoni 116
Gauguin, Paul 15, 17, 49, 53, 99, 100, 105, 112
Gawinski, Antoni 102
George, V L *126*
Georgi, Walter 77
Gibson, C D *129*
Gioia, Edoardo 43
Gipkens, J 83
Glass, Franz Paul 80
Glenny, A R 119
Goncharova, Natalia 106
Gottlieb, Leopold 102
Grabar, Igor 106
Grasset, Eugène 9, 13, 18-22, *18-20*, 41, 94-5, 106,

128

Gray, Henry (Henri Boulanger) 12, *14*
Greenaway, Kate 20
Gropius, Walter 71, 83
Group of Seven 111
Grün, Jules Alexandre *21, 23*
Gual i Queralt, Adrià 117
Gude, Hans 109
Guimard, Hector 8-9

Habich, Ludwig 83
Hamsun, Knut 108
Hankar, Paul 60, 64
Hansen, Emil 112
Hansen, Frida 109
Hardy, Dudley 28, *28-30*
Hassall, John 35, *38*
Heckel, E and Kirchner, E L 86
Heine, Thomas Theodor 67, 73, *73*, 77, 105, 106
Herald, James Watterston 35
Heubner, Friedrich 80
Hirth, George 67
Hodler, Ferdinand 86, 87-8
Hoffmann, Josef 88, 89, 90, 91, 92
Hohenstein, Adolfo, 41, *41-2*, 43
Hohlwein, Ludwig, *74, 76*, 77, *77-8*
Hokusai, Katsushika 10, 16
Holmboe, Othar *107*, 109
Holmboe, Thorolf 109
Horta, Victor 57
Housman, Laurence 35
Hüber, Patriz 83
Huyot, Jean-Georges *see* Auriol, Georges

Ibels, Henri Gabriel 16, *17*
Ibsen, Henrik 110
Image, Selwyn 30, 35
interior design *see* furniture and interiors
Italian Renaissance 33, 35

Jank, Angelo 77, *79*
Japanese influences: America 120, 132; Austria-Hungary 86; Belgium 53; France 9-10, 24; Great Britain 29, 33; Italy 42; Scandinavia 109; Spain 116
Jastrzebowski, Wojciech 102
Jensen-Hjell, Karl 108
Jones, Owen 120
Jonsach, Wilhelm *85, 90*
Juell, Dagny 109
Jugend 67, 73, 77, 101-2
Jugendstil 67-8, 70, 101

Kandinsky, Vassily 72, 106
Karelian movement 110
Kedzierski, Apoloniusz 102
Keene, N 29
Key, Ellen 111
Khnopff, Fernand 64
King, Jessie Marion 37-8
Kirchner, E L *see* Heckel and Kirchner

Klimt, Gustav 86-9, 90
Klinger, Julius 90, *90*
Klinger, Max 67, 87, 109
Knowles, M *121*
Köge, Wilhelm 111
Kokoschka, Oskar 89, 94
Kollwitz, Käthe 109
Korovin, Konstantin 105, 106
Krämer, Johann Viktor 89
Kreuger, Nils 112
Kupka, Frantisek 95
Kuznetsov, Pavel 106

Laerum, G 109, *110*
La Farge, John 119
Lalique, René 9
Lanceray, Evgenii 105
Landry, Abel 10
Larionov, Mikhail 106
Larsson, Carl 111
Laskoff, Franz (François Laskowski) 42
Leistikow, Walter 67
Lemmen, Georges 31, 49, 64
Lenart, Bonawentura 102
Les XX 49, 53, 57, 64, 110
Leyendecker, Frank X 138
Leyendecker, Joseph Christian *129, 138*
Liebermann, Max 67, 109
Lilien, Ephraim 102
Liljefors, Bruno 111
Livemont, Privat *59-60, 62, 64*
Löffler, Bertold 93
Long, F Y *123*
Loos, Adolf 94
Lundborg, F *120*

Mackintosh, Charles and Margaret *see* "The Four"
Mackmurdo, Arthur 30, 35
McNair, Herbert and Frances *see* "The Four"
Macquoid, Percy 31
Maiani, Augusto *see* Nàsica
Majorelle, Louis 9
Malczewski, Jacek 101
Mánes, Josef 95-6
Martini, Alberto 45
Massó i Torrents, Jaume 116
Mataloni, Giovanni 41-2, *41*
Maus, Octave 53
Mauzan, Achille 45
Mayreder, Julius 89
Mazza, Aldo 43
Mazzucotelli, Alessandro 45
Mehoffer, Jozef 100-1, 102
Meier-Graefe, Julius 7, 10, 46, 57, 68, 109
Mestres i Oños, Apelles 116
Métivet, Lucien 22
Metlicovitz, Leopoldo 42, *42*, 43
Meunier, Georges 12
Meunier, Henri *62-3*, 64
Meyer, Adolf 83

Michelazzi, Giovanni 45
Mir Iskusstva 34, 105-6
"Miriam" *see* Prezesmycki, Zenon
Molkenboer, Theodorus H A A 48, 51
Moll, Carl 88, 89, 93
Mondrian, Piet 49
Moore, Edward Chandler 120
Moreau, Gustave 102, 105
Moretti, Gaetano 45
Morris, Talwin 37
Morris, William 20, 28, 32, 38, 43, 49, 53, 57, 68, 100, 110, 111, 116
Moser, Koloman 84-5, 88, 89, 90-2
Mucha, Alphonse 21, 41, 42, 43, 45, 88-9, *91-6*, 96-7, 99, 100, 117
Munch, Edvard 67, 108-9
Munich Secession 67-8, 70, 72, 73, 77, 86, 106
Münter, Gabriele 106
Munthe, Gerhard 109
Münzer, Adolf, 99, 101
Muthesius, Hermann 83

Nabi group 15-16, 86, 96, 105
Nagy, Sándor 94
Nancy School 9
Nàsica (Augusto Maiani) 45
nature: America 120; France 22-3
Nesterov, Mikhail Vasilievich 104
Nicholson, Sir William *see* Beggarstaff Brothers
Niemeyer, Adalbert 73
Niesiolowski, Tymon 102
Nieuwenhuis, Theodor 51
Normann, Adelsten 109
Nuvel, Walter 105

Okun, Edward 102, *101*
Obrist, Hermann 64, 68, 83
Olbrich, Josef Maria 83, 87, *87*, 90
opera scores: Italy 41
Orazi, Manuel 46
Orlik, Emil 96

Palanti, Giuseppe 45
Pan 64-5, 68, 70, 102, 109, 110
Pankok, Bernhard 83
Parrish, Maxfield *133*, 136-8
Paul, Bruno *72*, 73, *73*, 83
Péan, René 12
Penfield, Edward 124, *127-8, 130*, 132-6
Peredvizhniki 104
Picard, Edmond 53
Piglheim, Bruno 72
Pogány, William Andrew (Willy) 95
posters: America 120-1, 124-5, 128-9; Austria-Hungary 94; Belgium 64-5; France 10-14, 20-1, 24-6; Germany 73, 77; Great Britain 31, 34-5; Italy 41-2; Russia 106; Spain 116
Powolny, Michael 93
Preisler, Jan 96
Preissig, Vojtech 96

143

Pre-Raphaelities 29, 36, 43, 45, 49, 64, 86, 88, 99, 116
Previati, Gaetano 45
Prikker, Johan Thorn 48, 49, *50*
printing and publishing: Spain 116
Procajlowicz, Antoni 102
Prouvé, Victor 9
Pryde, James *see* Beggarstaff Brothers
Przesmycki, Zenon ("Miriam") 102
Przybyszewski, Stanislaw 109
Puig i Cadafalch, Josep 116-17
Putz, Leo 77
Pyle, Howard 128, 132

Racken School 111
Rackham, Arthur 123
Ranson, Paul 16
Rassenfosse, Armand 65, 69
Réalier-Dumas, Maurice *22, 23*
Reed, Ethel *131*, 138
Rembowski, Jan 102
Rhead, Louis 129, *132, 135*, 136, *137*
Richardson, H H 119
Ricketts, Charles 35, *38*, 49, 121
Ricordi artists 41-3, 45
Riemerschmid, Richard 70, 83
Rigotti, Annibale 45
Rippl-Rónai, József 94
Riquer i Inglada, Alexandre 116-17
Rivière, Henri 16
Roerich, Nicholas 105
Roland Holst, Richard Nicolaus 49
Roller, Alfred 92
Roman Secession 43, 45
Romeu, Père 117
Rops, Félicien 65
Rosenberg, Lev *see* Bakst, Léon
Rossetti, Dante Gabriel 30, *32*, 41, 102
Rossi, Luigi 45
Roussel, Ker-Xavier 15
Rubino, Antonio 45
Ruchet, Bertha 68
Rusiñol i Prats, Santiago 116-17
Ruszczyc, Ferdynand 102
Ruty, Paul 95

Salons de la Rose+Croix 14, 16, 22, 64
Samokich-Soudkovskaya, Elena 106
Sant'Elia, Antonio 45
Sapunov, Nikolai 106
Sardou, Victorien 94
Sartorio, Aristide 43
Saryan, Martiros 106
Schelfhout, Lodewijk 49
Schiele, Egon 89
Schmidt, Karl 70, 83
Schwabe, Carlos 14, *15*, 36, 95
Segantini, Giovanni 45, 67
Serov, Valentin 105
Serrurier-Bovy, Gustave 53-6, 64
Sérusier, Paul 15

Sèthe, Maria 57
Seurat, Georges 53, 64, 105
Sezanne, Augusto *43*, 45
Shannon, Charles 35
Simberg, Hugo 111
Simplicissimus 44, 67, 73, 77
Siville, Maurice 65
Sjögren, Arthur 112
Skovgaard, Joachim 112
Slewinski, Waldyslaw 99-100
Sloan, John *132*, 138
Sluyters, J *53*
Sommaruga, Giuseppe 44
Somov, Konstantin 105-6
Sparre, Louis 110
Stabrowski, Kazimierz 102
Stämning painting 108
Steinlen, Théophile Alexandre 23, *23*, 105, 117
Stelletski, D S 106
Stilwell Weber, Sarah S 132
Stöhr, Ernest 89
Strathmann, Carl 73
Strindberg, August 109, 110
Stryjenski, Karol and Zofia 102
Studio, The 31, 33, 37, 41, 94, 105, 111
Sullam, Guido Constante 45
Sullivan, Louis 119
Surrealists 45
Symbolists 14-16, 49, 64, 86, 101, 102, 105, 111, 117; 'Blue Rose' group 106
Sztuka 99, 100, 102

Taylor, Ernest A 38
Terzi, Aleardo 43
"The Four" (Charles and Margaret Mackintosh, Herbert and Frances McNair) 36-7, *39*, 45, 83, 90-1, 123
Thiriet, Henri 23
Thoma, Hans 67
Tichy, Karol 100
Tiffany, Louis Comfort 119-23
Toorop, Jan 31, 37, *47*, 49, 73, 86, 101
Toulouse-Lautrec, Henri de 12, 16, *17*, 23-6, *23-6*, 53, 88, 106, 117, 121
Toussaint, Fernand 64
Trojanowski, Edward 100
Trübner, Wilhelm 67
Tschichold, Jan 123
Turbia-Krysztalowicz, Stanislaw 102
typography and book design: America 121, 123-4; Belgium 57; France 20; Germany 64, 72; Great Britain 28, 35; Italy 41-2; Poland 100; Russia 105

Utrillo i Morlius, Miquel 117
Utrillo i Viadera, Antoni 117

Vachal, Josef 96
Valentini, G 45
Vallotton, Félix 16, *17*, 102
van der Leck, Bart 51
van de Velde, Henry 7, 10, 31, 41, 49, *54-5, 56-7*,

64, 68, 83, 91, 109
van Gogh, Vincent 49, 53, 105
van Hoytema, Theo 51
van Rysselberghe, Théo *58*, 64
Vasnetsov, Victor 105
Vaszary, János 94
Vedder, Elihu 121
Ver Sacrum 84, 86, 91, 92
Vereinigte Werkstätten 68, 70, 71, 73
Verhaeren, Emile 49
Vienna Secession 22, 31, 37, 86-93, 102
Vigeland, Gustav 109
Villa, Aleardo 42-3
Viollet-Le-Duc, Eugène 8, 19, 20, 60, 119
Vogder, Heinrich 83
von Debschitz, Wilhelm 68
von Hoffmann, Ludwig 67, 83
von Matsch, Franz 86
Vonnoh, Robert 128
von Stuck, Franz 67, *71-2, 72-3*, 77
von Uhde, Fritz 67, 72
von Zügel, Heinrich 72
Vrubel, Mikhail Aleksandrovich 104-5
Vuillard, Edouard 15, 18

Wagner, Otto 88, 89, 90
Walker, Frederick 11, *11*
Weimarer Kunstgewerbeschule 57, 83
Weisgerber, Albert 77
Weiss, Wojciech 102
Whistler, James McNeill 25, 29, 33, 36, 138
Wiener Werkstätte 88, 90-1, 93
Wildt, Adolfo 45
Willette, Adolphe *21*, 23
Willumsen, Jens Ferdinand *111*, 112
Witzel, J 80
Wojtala, Franciszek 102
Wojtkiewicz, Witold 101, *102*
Wyspianski, Stanislaw 99-100, 102

Yakunchikova, Maria 104
Yavlensky, Alexei 106
Yellow Book, The 33-4, *33*, 121

Zecchin, Vittorio 45
Zorn, Anders 111

Index by Ann Edwards